Disconnected

The John D. and Catherine T. MacArthur Foundation Series on Digital Media and Learning

Engineering Play: A Cultural History of Children's Software, by Mizuko Ito

Hanging Out, Messing Around, and Geeking Out: Kids Living and Learning with New Media, by Mizuko Ito, Sonja Baumer, Matteo Bittanti, danah boyd, Rachel Cody, Becky Herr-Stephenson, Heather A. Horst, Patricia G. Lange, Dilan Mahendran, Katynka Martínez, C. J. Pascoe, Dan Perkel, Laura Robinson, Christo Sims, and Lisa Tripp, with contributions by Judd Antin, Megan Finn, Arthur Law, Annie Manion, Sarai Mitnick, David Schlossberg, and Sarita Yardi

The Civic Web: Young People, the Internet, and Civic Participation, by Shakuntala Banaji and David Buckingham

Connected Play: Tweens in a Virtual World, by Yasmin B. Kafai and Deborah A. Fields

The Digital Youth Network: Cultivating New Media Citizenship in Urban Communities, edited by Brigid Barron, Kimberley Gomez, Nichole Pinkard, and Caitlin K. Martin

Connected Code: Children as the Programmers, Designers, and Makers for the 21st Century, by Yasmin B. Kafai and Quinn Burke

Disconnected: Youth, New Media, and the Ethics Gap, by Carrie James

The Interconnections Collection: Understanding Systems through Digital Design, developed by Kylie Peppler, Melissa Gresalfi, Katie Salen Tekinbaş, and Rafi Santo

Gaming the System: Designing with Gamestar Mechanic, by Katie Salen Tekinbaş, Melissa Gresalfi, Kylie Peppler, and Rafi Santo

Script Changers: Digital Storytelling with Scratch, by Kylie Peppler, Rafi Santo, Melissa Gresalfi, and Katie Salen Tekinbaş

Short Circuits: Crafting E-Puppets with DIY Electronics, by Kylie Peppler, Katie Salen Tekinbaş, Melissa Gresalfi, and Rafi Santo

Soft Circuits: Crafting E-Fashion with DIY Electronics, by Kylie Peppler, Melissa Gresalfi, Katie Salen Tekinbaş, and Rafi Santo

Inaugural Series Volumes

Six edited volumes were created through an interactive community review process and published online and in print in December 2007. They are the precursors to the peer-reviewed monographs in the series. For more information on these volumes, visit http://mitpress.mit.edu/books/series/john-d-and-catherine-t-macarthur -foundation-series-digital-media-and-learning.

Disconnected

Youth, New Media, and the Ethics Gap

Carrie James

The MIT Press
Cambridge, Massachusetts
London, England

MIT Press books may be purchased at special quantity discounts for business or sales promotional use. For information, please email special_sales@mitpress.mit.edu.

This book was set in Stone by the MIT Press. Printed and bound in the United States of America.

Library of Congress Cataloging-in-Publication Data
James, Carrie.
Disconnected : youth, new media, and the ethics gap / Carrie James.
    pages   cm — (The John D. and Catherine T. Macarthur Foundation series on digital media and learning)
Includes bibliographical references and index.
ISBN 978-0-262-02806-6 (hardcover : alk. paper) — 978-0-262-52941-9 (pb.)
1. Internet and youth. 2. Internet—Moral and ethical aspects. 3. Parental influences. I. Title.
HQ799.9.I58J36   2014
004.67'80835—dc23
2014003873

10 9 8 7 6 5 4 3 2

For Ella and Talia, my young digital citizens

Every technology is both a burden and a blessing; not either-or, but this-and-that.
—Neil Postman[1]

Technology celebrates connectedness but encourages retreat.... The flow of water carves rock, a little bit at a time. And our personhood is carved, too, by the flow of our habits.... The more distracted we become, and the more emphasis we place on speed at the expense of depth, the less likely and able we are to care.

We often use technology to save time, but increasingly, it either takes the saved time along with it or makes the saved time less present, intimate, and rich. I worry that the closer the world gets to our fingertips, the farther it gets from our hearts. It's not an either/or—being "anti-technology" is perhaps the only thing more foolish than being unquestioningly "pro-technology"—but a question of balance that our lives hang upon.
—Jonathan Safran Foer[2]

Contents

Series Foreword

In recent years, digital media and networks have become embedded in our everyday lives and are part of broad-based changes in how we engage in knowledge production, communication, and creative expression. Unlike in the early years of the development of computers and computer-based media, digital media are now *commonplace* and *pervasive*, having been taken up by a wide range of individuals and institutions in all walks of life. Digital media have escaped the boundaries of professional and formal practice and of the academic, governmental, and industry homes that initially fostered their development. Now they have been taken up by diverse populations and in noninstitutionalized practices, including the peer activities of youth. Although the specific forms of technology uptake are highly diverse, a generation is growing up in an era when digital media are part of the taken-for-granted social and cultural fabric of learning, play, and social communication.

This book series is founded on the working hypothesis that those immersed in new digital tools and networks are engaged in an unprecedented exploration of language, games, social interaction, problem solving, and self-directed activity that leads to diverse forms of learning. These diverse forms of learning are reflected in expressions of identity, in how individuals express independence and creativity, and in their ability to learn, exercise judgment, and think systematically.

The defining frame for this series is not a particular theoretical or disciplinary approach, nor is it a fixed set of topics. Rather, the series revolves around a constellation of topics investigated from multiple disciplinary and practical frames. The series as a whole looks at the relation among youth, learning, and digital media, but each contribution to the series might deal with only a subset of this constellation. Erecting strict topical boundaries would exclude some of the most important work in the field. For example, restricting the content of the series only to people of a certain age would mean artificially reifying an age boundary when the phenomenon demands otherwise. This would become particularly problematic with new forms of online participation in which an important outcome is the mixing of participants of different ages. The same goes for digital media, which are increasingly inseparable from analog and earlier media forms.

This series responds to certain changes in our media ecology that have important implications for learning. Specifically, these changes involve new forms of media *literacy* and developments in the modes of media *participation*. Digital media are part of a convergence between interactive media (most notably gaming), online networks, and existing media forms. Navigating this media ecology involves a palette of literacies that are being defined through practice but that require more scholarly scrutiny before they can be fully incorporated into educational initiatives. Media literacy involves not only ways of understanding, interpreting, and critiquing media but also the means for creative and social expression, online search and navigation, and a host of new technical skills. The potential gap in literacies and participation skills creates new challenges for educators who struggle to bridge media engagement inside and outside the classroom.

The John D. and Catherine T. MacArthur Foundation Series on Digital Media and Learning, published by the MIT Press, aims to close these gaps and provide innovative ways of thinking about and using new forms of knowledge production, communication, and creative expression.

Foreword: What *Were* They Thinking?

Henry Jenkins

We know the rules of community; we know the healing effect of community in terms of individual lives.... We human beings have often been referred to as social animals. But we are not yet community creatures. We are impelled to relate with each other for our survival. But we do not yet relate with the inclusivity, realism, self-awareness, vulnerability, commitment, openness, freedom, equality, and love of genuine community. It is clearly no longer enough to be simply social animals, babbling together at cocktail parties and brawling with each other in business and over boundaries. It is our task—our essential, central, crucial task—to transform ourselves from mere social creatures into community creatures.
—M. Scott Peck, *The Different Drum: Community-Making and Peace*, p. 165

A working-class black woman lingered after I spoke about youth and digital media at Detroit's Wayne State University. She pushed her way through the crowd to ask a simple question: "Will my boy be all right?"

Her adolescent son spent a great deal of time online: talking with friends, building his home page, playing computer games, doing his homework. She had heard conflicting reports—teachers claiming Internet access fostered educational growth, and media reformers warning about teens "running amok" online. Like so many other parents, she worried that she was wrong to let her son explore cyberspace when she knew so little about computers herself. She feared that she did not know enough to give him the guidance he needed and wondered if perhaps the only answer was to unplug the expensive device she had brought into her home.

This is one of many such encounters I've had with parents and youth (of all races and economic backgrounds) through the years, as people asked some core questions about whether these new media platforms and practices are helping to make us better or worse people. Many parents have asked whether their children would be all right and often have looked at particular choices their sons and daughters had made online, asking, "What *were* they thinking?"

I've often wished I could give them a book like *Disconnected* to read—a book that does not respond with fear and panic but instead speaks directly about how we might foster more responsible digital citizens and encourage healthier online communities. Over six years, a team of 14 researchers at Harvard's Good Play Project interviewed young people—teens, tweens, and young adults—about their digital lives, the ethical challenges they face online, and the values that govern the choices they make about how to treat people they encounter on social media. What emerges here is a complex picture—one that sees these emerging platforms and practices as "not either-or, but this-and-that," both a "burden" and a "blessing" (Postman 1993, 5). Some of what Carrie James shares about young people's ethical choices may alarm us, some may give us hope, but, most of all, the book reveals what many of us have come to recognize—the online world is neither an ideal society nor hell on earth. Rather, the online world is a place where we conduct routine aspects of our daily lives, and often we think less than we should about the consequences of the choices we are making there.

As I've read this book, I've found myself thinking about its evocative title, about the various ways we might describe American youth as "disconnected," even as they are more heavily wired than previous generations. Some of them are disconnected from any kind of online community, having little to no understanding of the participatory mechanisms or shared norms that apply to different forms of online social interactions. Some of them see little to no connection between what they do online and what gets valued by their parents or schools. Some seem not to be able to meaningfully connect what they do online with the consequences of their actions on others or to connect digital avatars with the flesh-and-blood people whose feelings may be hurt by their hateful words and actions. Some have little or no connection to adults who might provide them with meaningful insight into the situations they encounter, and some have no real access to older ethical and spiritual traditions as they make decisions that can sometimes have serious implications for their lives and the lives of others.

Carrie James states early in the book that she is offering a "glass half empty" perspective:

I harbor real concerns about the local and global consequences, often hidden, of the uncivil, cruel, and harmful conduct that is common, if not routine, in some online communities. I worry that such conduct discourages participating, thus undercutting one of the central promises of the Internet. I also worry about the general lack of attention to moral and ethical concerns on the Internet, compared with the emphasis on personal safety issues. (21)

I share those concerns, even though I am a "glass half full" guy. James and I would agree, however, that we are still looking at half a glass and that more needs to be done to support our young people's moral development in the digital age. I care very much about the issues James raises here because I believe that our goal should be to expand who has access to the means of cultural production, circulation, and participation. The best way to realize those potentials is to soberly assess and meaningfully address the roadblocks we encounter along the path toward a more participatory culture.

In the beginning, some of us hoped that venturing into the online world would encourage people to reflect on the nature of our relationships with each other, experiment with new kinds of social arrangements, experience new kinds of collective identities, and, through that process, bring a renewed sense of social connectivity back into the realm of everyday experience. These ideals are suggested by the above passage from M. Scott Peck, which Howard Rheingold used as the epigraph for his 1993 book, *The Virtual Community: Homesteading on the Electronic Frontier.* There, Rheingold (2000, vii) summed up the hopes and ideals of the first generation of what we used to call "netizens"—chief among them, the wish that digital media would offer tools we could use to "transform ourselves from mere social creatures into community creatures."

Rheingold based his concept of "the virtual community" on his own experiences within the Well, an early BBS (bulletin-board system) widely understood as a site of experimentation and reflection on the social affordances of networked computing. Fred Turner (2006) has seen the Well as emblematic of the transition "from counterculture to cyberculture," as many of those who helped to define the new digital culture did so from a perspective informed by 1960s- and 1970s-era experiments with gift economies, participatory democracy, and communitarianism. The Well saw itself as diverse, bringing together many who did not know each other face to face. Compared to what the Web would become, however, the Well was surprisingly local, given most of the participants came from the Bay Area and were part of the professional classes of early Web adopters. Kevin Driscoll (2014) situates the Well as a highly visible example of thousands of local networks that were using these emerging technologies as a way to reimagine American social life. Initially, these groups were so grounded in local cultures that there was no need to articulate their shared values, ideals, or norms. But, as they began to diversify, there were widespread efforts to codify "netiquette," to put into words what they hoped to achieve together and to define shared expectations about appropriate ways of dealing with their differences.

Today, there is a tendency to think of these early netizens as naive utopianists. Yet, if we look more closely, we will see that they were well aware of the problems that humans brought with them into the digital realm and understood the likelihood that they were going to botch this opportunity for reinventing themselves and their society. Howard Rheingold (2000, xxx) spells out the stakes: "We temporarily have access to a tool that could bring conviviality and understanding into our lives and might help revitalize the public sphere. The same tool, improperly controlled and wielded, could become an instrument of tyranny." Which outcome emerged would depend on active choices made by those participating within these online communities; Rheingold (2000, 306) stressed "the hard work that must be done in real life to harvest the fruits of that democratizing power."

These were not the words of a technological determinist: there was no inevitability here that these technologies would necessarily serve a democratizing function. Connectivity was understood as a property of the technologies we used, but a potential that also depended on a set of social norms that netizens struggled to define as they learned to create shared experiences together. These netizens were seeking online the sense of belonging that once characterized small town American life, even as social critics of the period argued that such social connections had been lost forever within a contemporary society where people did not know, let alone care about, their neighbors.

Another early writer about digital culture, Julian Dibbell (1993), documented some of the important conversations about self-governance and ethical norms within these early "virtual communities." Writing about an early MUD, LambdaMOO, Dibbell described an incident where "Mr. Bungle" committed an act of "virtual rape" or sexual harassment (depending on your perspective) on the avatar of a female participant, forcing the community to come together and decide how they were going to deal with this antisocial behavior:

Since getting the wizards to toad Mr. Bungle (or to toad the likes of him in the future) required a convincing case that the cry for his head came from the community at large, then the community itself would have to be defined; and if the community was to be convincingly defined, then some form of social organization, no matter how rudimentary, would have to be settled on. And thus, as if against its will, the question of what to do about Mr. Bungle began to shape itself into a sort of referendum on the political future of the MOO.

The Mr. Bungle incident quickly entered the mythology of the early Web, a signpost of the ways that people with good will and high ideals might work things out together.

And many hoped that young people who came of age interacting with each other within such online communities might embody a new set of social norms and values. Don Tapscott's book, *Growing Up Digital*, described those aspirations as if they had already been achieved:

They are the young navigators. They doubt that traditional institutions can provide them with the good life and take personal responsibility for their lives. They do value material goods but they are not self-absorbed. They are more knowledgeable than any previous generation, and they care deeply about social issues. They believe strongly in individual rights such as privacy and rights to information. But they have no ethos of individualism, thriving, rather, from close interpersonal networks and displaying a strong sense of social responsibility. (Tapscott 1998, 9)

We all wanted so much to believe this to be true, though *Disconnected* offers a somewhat more conflicted account of how young people are working through many of these same issues today.

During that same time period, I would still encounter many of these same ideals when I studied what young people had to say about (and on) their home pages. I argued that young people felt strongly about their home pages precisely because they lacked control in their physical environments—they were seeking some way to create a space where they could get in touch with their better selves. They often characterized the Web as:

a refuge from divorced parents, economic hardship, crowded classrooms, intolerant teachers, and hostile peers. As one raver said of his site, "This place, my little home on the Web, was designed out of the desire to have a place to go when I want to feel like there are no problems, no worries, no stress and no violence in or around my life" Another girl named her Web site "Palisades," explaining the word's relevance: "A strong fence made of stakes driven into the ground for defense. Palisades is a place where I can feel free to express myself without fear of being torn down.... Within the Palisades you will find the real me." (Jenkins 2001)

Such idealistic statements about digital culture stood in stark contrast to the ways that young people's digital lives were being pathologized in mainstream media, where parents were being taught to fear what young people might encounter if they spent too much time at their computers. Medical authorities were urging parents to move the computer out of the teen's bedrooms and into publically visible spaces to see if greater parental oversight might diminish their likelihood for mischief, cyberbullying, illegal downloads, violent gaming, or porn consumption.

At the time, it was as if there were only two ways to perceive the Web—as a space of personal freedom and enlightenment or as a space of darkness and risk. And those of us who wanted to defend what we valued about the online world had few choices except to push back against what we saw as a moral panic about digital technology, a case of adults not understanding a world that had not been part of their own childhood experiences. We were motivated by the knowledge that there was a whole generation of youth who were becoming media makers, expressing their emerging understanding of the world through fan fiction, game mods, MP3 recordings, websites, videos, social network site profiles, digital photographs, and a wealth of other grassroots production practices. As they did so, some (though not all) of them were stepping into support systems around what we call participatory culture. They were using these technologies to construct their identities, make sense of their social interactions with their peers, and gain respect from adults who shared their goals and backgrounds. Some of them were joining online communities that, at their best, met their needs, but, in other cases, failed them. These youth had access to much greater communicative power than previous generations could have imagined, and they were using this power in both constructive and destructive ways.

This perspective led me to coauthor a 2006 white paper, "Confronting the Challenges of Participatory Culture," which was published as a kind of manifesto to accompany the launch of the MacArthur Foundation's Digital Media and Learning initiative. In that report, we identified "The Ethics Challenge," alongside "The Participation Gap" and "The Transparency Problem," as three core issues media literacy instructors needed to confront if they were going to prepare young people to meaningfully engage with the new media landscape. Our perspective on ethics was very much informed by research produced by Harvard's Good Work Project. We wrote:

One important goal of media education should be to encourage young people to become more reflective about the ethical choices they make as participants and communicators and about the impact they have on others. In the short run, we may have to accept that cyberspace's ethical norms are in flux: we are taking part in a prolonged experiment in what happens when barriers of entry into a communication landscape become lower. For the present moment, asking and working through questions of ethical practices may be more valuable than the answers produced because the process will help everyone to recognize and articulate the different assumptions that guide their behavior. (Jenkins et al. 2009, 26)

I first met Carrie James as Howard Gardner (her mentor) and I sought to bring together our two research teams—Harvard's Good Play Project (an outgrowth of the Good Work Project) and MIT's New Media Literacies Project—to work together to produce a set of educational resources we felt would encourage educators, parents, and youth to reflect about the ethical choices they make in their everyday engagements online. We called the project *Our Space: Being a Responsible Citizen of the Digital World* (The Good Play Project and Project New Media Literacies 2011). Carrie James was the point person at the Good Play Project with whom our group interfaced. We became effective thinking partners and collaborators, in large part because we did not come at these issues from the same perspective.

True to stereotypes about our respective institutions, the MIT team was more optimistic about the potentials of forging new kinds of communities in cyberspace, whereas the Harvard team was more skeptical about the issues associated with abandoning older, valuable practices or about the risks that young people face in an increasingly commercialized online world. The Harvard team was mostly drawn from the fields of education and psychology, with the consequence that they tended to focus on individuals and their personal experiences, whereas the MIT team tended to come from communications or cultural studies, fields much more focused on collective experiences and shared social norms. As a consequence, we balanced each other, forcing each group to defend its perspectives and test its assumptions, and we produced a project that could be used by teachers who also came at these topics from a range of different angles (published after our project had relocated to USC). More recently, my team has once again joined forces with Carrie James, Howard Gardner, and others from the Good Play Project as part of the MacArthur Foundation's Youth and Participatory Politics Research Network, a multidisciplinary group of scholars seeking to better understand the civic and political lives of American youth, online and off.

Coming out of these experiences together, I was deeply honored to be asked to write this foreword. Through the years, I have come to value James as someone who brings a valuable perspective to these conversations—skeptical, yes, but also open-minded and pragmatic. I have learned a tremendous amount from our interactions through the years—perhaps, most powerfully, the difference between focusing on the youth who are most immersed in participatory culture and most effective at deploying new media platforms and practices toward their own ends and focusing on those youth who have limited access or imperfect understandings of these communities and their traditions.

Thanks to the leadership the MacArthur Foundation has provided in seeking to build a multidisciplinary field around digital media and learning, there have been countless case studies that show us the benefits of learning within a participatory culture, and we've seen some progress made by schools, museums, libraries, and other public institutions to model themselves after what works in these online "affinity spaces." James's research here confirms our earlier intuitions: those youth who are actively engaged in interest-driven networks that encourage self-reflection about the nature of online participation have a clearer sense of shared ethical norms than those who are encountering the complexities of an emerging digital culture on their own. But, as recent reports from the MacArthur Foundation Digital Media and Learning Hub's Connected Learning initiative (Ito et al. 2013) have indicated, there has also been a growing recognition that access to those spaces, even knowledge of their existence, is unevenly distributed and that most young people lack strong mentors who can help them work through the challenges they confront online and who can guide them into forms of digital participation that might prove meaningful.

Young people do not need adults snooping over their shoulders and intruding into their online lives, but they do need adults who will watch their backs and provide them with the insights and resources they need to make meaningful choices. When we look closely at parental attitudes toward new media, we still see a tendency toward prohibitionism and moral panic and an emphasis on how to avoid risks, which are often understood primarily in terms of their impact on the individual child rather than in the framework of a larger community and which are addressed by seeking to block or limit access to technological resources without regard to the social, educational, economic, and civic benefits of participating in these communities. Other adults display attitudes of indifference or permissiveness, convinced that youth will "sort these things out on their own, as they always have." Still others see young people's online experiences as a "waste of time." Such attitudes discourage the kinds of deep reflection many of us think is necessary. When many young people tell us that what they do online "really doesn't matter," they are simply mirroring adults who have trivialized their digital lives. Attitudes which position digital culture as totally new, and without precedent, may also have the consequence of cutting youth off from older sources of wisdom, of leaving adults feeling like their common sense and basic moral impulses count for little when helping young people deal with their online lives.

So, the first step in building a stronger ethical context for talking about young people's digital lives is to take those experiences seriously, seeing the choices youth are making as important in terms of defining who they are now and who they will become in the future. Writers like Shakuntala Banaji and David Buckingham (2013), danah boyd (2014), and Lynn Scofield Clark (2012)—as well as Sonia Livingstone (2009), S. Craig Watkins (2009), and other members of the Connected Learning network—have played valuable roles in those debates. I see *Disconnected* as very much within that same tradition, a highly nuanced picture of how young people are confronting the challenges of everyday life in the digital era.

If the Good Play research reveals some core concerns that we all need to address, I also read the book as challenging some of the smug assumptions adults make, such as the idea that young people no longer care about issues of privacy or that young people have no moral concerns about illegal downloads. This book shows us young people who are struggling to resolve core contradictions in their thinking about privacy, publicity, participation, and property within cyberspace. These youth may not think about these issues in the same ways that some adults want them to do, but they do care about these issues deeply, and many of them are making much more nuanced choices than has previously been suggested.

Drawing insights both from the Good Play Project's extended interviews and from the literature on moral development in children and adolescents, James identifies a range of different moral philosophies that shape how young people think about these issues. What these youth told the researchers allows James to map the complex moral reasoning through which young people arrive at tactical solutions that help them to get through their day-to-day interactions online. We see examples of how they work through competing ethical norms, and we see evidence that their choices reflect differing states of social development, as they acquire more complete understandings of the world around them and their place within it. What quickly becomes clear is that these young people do not in any meaningful sense constitute a generation of "digital natives," fully at home in cyberspace, and that there is no such thing as a digital mindset, at least not one unified perspective or disposition through which they make sense of their online experiences. Rather, these young people's online lives are more fragmented, contradictory and—yes, more disconnected than such models would suggest.

James closes the book with an urgent plea for what she calls "Conscientious Connectivity," defined variously as "an ethical disposition toward the digital world, ... the use of ethical thinking skills, a sensitivity to the moral and ethical dimensions of online situation, and a motivation to reflect on and wrestle with the associated dilemmas, ... a sense of agency in relation to the integrity of the Web" (109). Is "conscientious connectivity" something we carry within us as we move from one digital platform to the next, or is it something that takes root within specific communities as they reflect on their own norms and practices, as Rheingold and other early theorists of digital culture had hoped? Should we be surprised that the kinds of participatory culture emerging within communities that have long traditions of collaborative creativity often foster a greater consciousness around some of these issues than typical discussions in the comments section of a site like YouTube, where participants all too often are deeply hostile to any and all forms of diversity? What happens at the intersections between these various communities of shared interests and practices, as they brush up against each other in shared spaces where communal commitments are not promoted or policed? Should the burden of fostering these skills rest on individual classroom teachers, parents, and mentors? Is this something young people should develop on their own? Is this something we value enough to bring into all of the key institutions—from public libraries to churches, from scout troops to museums—which impact young people's developing sense of their own moral character?

Early writers like Rheingold or Dibbell assumed that such opportunities for ethical reflection would appear spontaneously as we all adjusted to the challenges of conducting our social lives in these unfamiliar ways, as new forms of social organization leveraged the affordances of many-to-many communications and lowered transaction costs, as we sought to make real the promises we associated with concepts such as *virtual community* or *participatory culture*. Some youth are still encountering such conversations as they engage in interest-based networks. But, as the Web has become routinized, and as interacting with others in digital places and spaces no longer seems surprising or unfamiliar, we've seen far too few opportunities to reflect together on what kind of world is emerging here. As massive numbers of people are moving through these sites, it becomes harder to inculcate participants into their shared norms and ethical traditions. As we communicate with people around the world who we will never encounter face-to-face, it becomes harder to rely on shared values that we carry with us from our offline lives together, and, often, it becomes harder for us to feel empathetic toward others we encounter under these circumstances. Yet, at the same time, as more and more young people interact through social network sites primarily with people they already know offline, we are also more apt to play out hurts and conflicts from offline on digital platforms that amplify and archive our communications, and, thus, we have greater ability to inflict lasting and highly visible harm. Where young people sometimes saw the Web as a refuge from the harassment they faced in their offline lives at one time, there now seems to be no escape. And, as market norms often displace communitarian values—and as civic spaces give way to commercial spaces—it becomes harder to promote values other than "what's mine is mine" (20). The problem is that, contrary to the M. Scott Peck quote that began this foreword, it's not clear we "know the rules of community" online.

In this context, there's an urgent need for "conscientious connectivity": we can and must do better. I hope that *Disconnected* will be a springboard for important conversations we should be having about what principles should govern our understanding of digital citizenship and ethics. While the data contained here can helpfully inform such conversations, allowing adults a better understanding of what young people are thinking about their online lives, the ideal conversation will be cross-generational, as young and old ask each other probing questions and provide honest answers about what they are doing online and why.

References

Banaji, Shakuntala, and David Buckingham. 2013. *The Civic Web: Young People, the Internet, and Civic Participation*. Cambridge, MA: MIT Press.

boyd, danah. 2014. *It's Complicated: The Social Lives of Networked Teens*. New Haven: Yale University Press.

Clark, Lynn Scofield. 2012. *The Parent App: Understanding Families in the Digital Age*. New York: Oxford University Press.

Dibbell, Julian. 1993. A Rape in Cyberspace. *The Village Voice*, December 21. http://www.juliandibbell.com/texts/bungle_vv.html.

Driscoll, Kevin. 2014. *Hobbyist Inter-networking and the Popular Internet Imaginary: Forgotten Histories of Networked Personal Computing, 1978–1998*. PhD diss., Annenberg School of Communication and Journalism, University of Southern California.

The Good Play Project and Project New Media Literacies. 2011. *Our Space: Being a Responsible Citizen of the Digital World*. http://www.newmedialiteracies.org/our-space-being-a-responsible-citizen-of-the-digital-world.

Ito, Mitzuko, Kris Gutiérrez, Sonia Livingstone, Bill Penuel, Jean Rhodes, Katie Salen, Juliet Schor, Julian Sefton-Green, and S. Craig Watkins. 2013. Connected Learning: An Agenda for Research and Design. MacArthur Foundation Digital Media and Learning Research Hub Report on Connected Learning. http://dmlhub.net/sites/default/files/ConnectedLearning_report.pdf.

Jenkins, Henry. 2001. "The Kids Are All Right Online." *Technology Review*, January 1. http://www.technologyreview.com/article/400852/the-kids-are-all-right-online.

Jenkins, Henry, with Ravi Purushatma, Margaret Weigel, Katie Clinton, and Alice Robison. 2009. *Confronting the Challenges of Participatory Culture: Media Education for the 21st Century*. Cambridge, MA: MIT Press. http://mitpress.mit.edu/sites/default/files/titles/free_download/9780262513623_Confronting_the_Challenges.pdf. [Originally published in 2006]

Livingstone, Sonia. 2009. *Children and the Internet*. Malden, MA: Polity.

Peck, M. Scott. 1987. *The Different Drum: Community-Making and Peace*. New York: Touchstone.

Postman, Neil. 1993. *Technopoly: The Surrender of Culture to Technology*. New York: Vintage Books.

Rheingold, Howard. 2000. *The Virtual Community: Homesteading on the Electronic Frontier*. Rev. ed. Cambridge, MA: MIT Press. [Originally published in 1993]

Tapscott, Don. 1998. *Growing Up Digital: The Rise of the Net Generation.* New York: McGraw-Hill.

Turner, Fred. 2006. *From Counterculture to Cyberculture: Stewart Brand, the Whole Earth Network, and the Rise of Digital Utopianism.* Chicago: University of Chicago Press.

Watkins, S. Craig. 2009. *The Young and the Digital: What the Migration to Social Network Sites, Games and Anytime, Anywhere Media Means for Our Future.* Boston: Beacon Press.

Acknowledgments

This book would not have been possible without the support and encouragement of so many people.

I am especially grateful to Howard Gardner, with whom I've been fortunate to be able to work for more than 10 years. Howard has been a key mentor, supporter, and invaluable sounding board every step of the way. The project on which this book is based would never have happened without him, and this book is stronger for his keen insights and suggestions.

I am also indebted to Katie Davis, an incredible research partner and friend, whose insightful comments and moral support have been essential throughout the writing of this book. My close colleague, Margaret Rundle, has also been a great voice of encouragement and an insightful reader of my earliest draft chapters. I am thankful as well to Liz Dawes Duraisingh, Justin Reich, and Emily Weinstein for reading and sharing invaluable constructive criticism on specific thematic chapters.

I also owe thanks to my Project Zero colleague, Shari Tishman, for her general support and for help in exploring the links between the ideas in this book and the literature on thinking dispositions. As I wrote this book, I often thought of my undergraduate mentor, James Spates, who first piqued my curiosity about the nature of the good and whose ideas continue to inspire me.

I am so thankful to have been able to work with an amazing group of researchers over the life of the Good Play Project, from the early stages of informant interviews and data collection to the last stages of coding, analysis, and writing. I am so appreciative of the great contributions of Jessica Benjamin, James Croft, Katie Davis, Andrea Flores, John M. Francis, Sam Gilbert, Erhardt Graeff, Julie Maier, Lindsay Pettingill, Margaret Rundle, Je Oxman Ryan, and Margaret Weigel.

The voices of young people are an essential part of this book. I am thankful to all of the youth who shared their experiences, insights, and perspectives with us. Our interviews with parents and teachers were also incredibly valuable. It would have been difficult to carry out our study without the help of educators who welcomed us into their schools and organizations and connected us with youth, parents, and teachers. I am especially thankful to Michael Hannah, who was a source of input and support over many years of our project.

Susan Buckley and Katie Helke of the MIT Press provided great advice at various stages of this book project, from the development of the proposal through the final revisions of the manuscript; I am also very thankful to Deborah Cantor-Adams and Judith Antonelli for their terrific editorial support. I also benefited from insightful comments and suggestions given by anonymous reviewers of the book proposal and manuscript.

I am very grateful to Connie Yowell and An-Me Chung of the John D. and Catherine T. MacArthur Foundation for their support of our work. The Good Play Project team is fortunate to have been an early part of the foundation's Digital Media and Learning initiative. Over the years, my thinking about the ideas in this book has been informed by generative conversations with collaborators in and critical friends of the Digital Media and Learning network, including Sasha Barab, Linda Burch, Anne Collier, Mimi Ito, Henry Jenkins, Barry Joseph, Shira Katz, John Palfrey, Rafi Santo, and Sinem Siyahhan.

I've been incredibly lucky to have the full support of my close friends and family throughout the writing process. Tiffany Winne has been a constant presence, providing invaluable support from afar, cheering me on from the idea stage up through the very last set of revisions. Her friendship is a precious 30-year old gift that just keeps on giving. I've also been buoyed by the advice and encouragement of my longtime friends (and fellow sociologists and anthropologists) Karen Albright, Johanna Crane, and Tina Fetner. I'm thankful as well to Leah Barcan, my sister Emily James, Jessica Madison Ormsby, and Christy Snider for their support and for helping me celebrate the milestones along the way. Jon and Joan Grossman also offered words of encouragement throughout.

My mother, Judith Lowitz, was a tremendous source of support. Among other things, she and my stepfather, Nick Lowitz, provided invaluable help in taking care of my young daughters whenever I asked in order to give me long stretches of writing time. And one couldn't ask for a better partner than Perry Grossman—invaluable reader of the manuscript, thoughtful sounding board, super dad, and all-around great guy. This book never would have happened without his support. Finally, I am so grateful to my daughters, Ella and Talia, for their love, patience, and willingness to let me go to work, even on the weekends, so that I could write this book. I hope it makes them proud.

1 Morality, Ethics, and Digital Life

Three Cases

In September 2010, Rutgers University student Tyler Clementi committed suicide by jumping off the George Washington Bridge in New York City. In the wake of his death, it came to light that his roommate, Dharun Ravi, had covertly set up a webcam on two separate occasions to view Clementi having sexual relations with a male partner. Moreover, via Twitter, Ravi had invited friends to the viewings and posted commentary. In March 2012, Ravi was convicted of privacy invasion and bias intimidation, both criminal offenses. In a public statement issued by his lawyer, Ravi apologized for the "thoughtless, insensitive, immature, stupid, and childish choices ... which at no time were motivated by hate, bigotry, prejudice, or desire to hurt, humiliate, or embarrass anyone."[1]

In early 2011, Helene Hegemann, just 17 years old, entered the spotlight of the German literary world after publishing her novel, *Axolotl Roadkill*. The book was met with critical praise and was quickly nominated for a prestigious literary prize. However, within a month of the book's publication, accusations surfaced that Hegemann had lifted text, including almost an entire page of writing, from another writer's novel. In the controversy that ensued, Hegemann apologized but also justified her actions as creative "remixing," referring to herself as part of new generation of creators for whom "there's no such thing as originality ... just authenticity."[2]

In the fall of 2011, it came to light that a group of New York City police officers had created a Facebook group to vent with colleagues about patrol duty for the West Indian Day Parade, an annual event in Brooklyn. Posts on the public page referred to parade participants as "savages" and "animals." Comments included "Drop a bomb and wipe them all out" and "Let them kill each other." The Facebook group, named "No More West Indian Day Detail," had approximately 1,200 members. Sixty active participants' names matched the names of known police officers; other participants were described as "civilians and other city workers, including NYC firemen." The group was discovered by lawyers investigating an unrelated incident involving an officer who was an active participant in the group. The lawyers made a digital copy of the content before the page was deleted by a member. Ultimately, 17 police officers faced disciplinary action by the New York Police Department.[3]

Invaded privacy, stolen words, racist speech—offenses such as these have existed in human life for eons. Yet when they are committed in networked publics in a globally interconnected world, the stakes are arguably higher, the harm arguably deeper or at least more lasting. In this book, I explore troubling cases like these, as well as less dramatic digital dilemmas, to reveal the moral and ethical dimensions of the interconnected lives we now lead.

Central to this exploration are the ways of thinking that young people develop and hold about online situations, especially those involving privacy, property, and participation. I focus primarily on young people because they are often early adopters of new technologies and leading participants in many online settings, particularly social networks. Moreover, as Don Tapscott put it, youth are "growing up digital."[4] Thus, their identities and moral and ethical sensibilities are being fundamentally shaped by the new conditions of life, both positive and negative, wrought by digital media.

What does it mean to grow up in a world in which privacy is fragile and publicity can be used as a weapon to mock, humiliate, or punish another person? In which ownership and authorship are being contested by new affordances for remixing, repurposing, and just plain stealing? In which anonymous or at least arm's length mechanisms for spreading cruelty and hatred are so widely available? All these questions can certainly be posed in ways that accentuate the positive features and implications of the Web. The prosocial, civic, and political promises of the Internet are widely discussed and, studies suggest, realized to varying degrees. But the picture is incomplete if we don't also understand how the negative potentials and realities are experienced, are made sense of, and influence the moral and ethical dispositions of young people.

The three cases described above point to new potentials for harm—at both the individual and the group level—that accompany social media sites in particular and digital technologies in general. They also suggest the importance of exploring the ways of thinking that lead some young people, and adults, to dubious online acts. Dharun Ravi characterized his choices as "thoughtless" and "insensitive" but not intended to cause Clementi emotional duress. Helene Hegemann conceived of her use of another writer's words as a creative act, not as an intentional design to steal and present another's words as her own. Although the thinking of the police officers involved in the West Indian Day Parade Facebook group is not known, it's probably not a leap to imagine that they thought little, if at all, about the public nature of the content they posted or about their roles and responsibilities as police officers. From the officers' comments themselves, it is evident that at least one participant believed that the complaints were justifiable or at least not racist. "It's not racist if it's true," he posted.[5]

The ways of thinking evident to various degrees in these cases have a few noteworthy features. First, at least on the part of Ravi and Hegemann, there is a suggested lack of intentionality to cause harm. Related to this, and evident in all three cases, is an obvious failure to consider the potential effects of one's actions on other people, known and unknown. The latter is a considerable failure in light of the networked, public nature of the contexts in which our actions are often situated in the digital age. Throughout the book, I describe such thinking shortfalls as *blind spots* and *disconnects*. Overall, I argue that blind spots and disconnects are common to an unfortunate degree in mediated communication—when we interact, play, collaborate, and share content and ideas via text message, email, social media, and other virtual means.

Drawing on qualitative interviews with young people ages 10–25, I explore the extent to which, and how, such thinking shortfalls are evident when the individuals talk about their digital lives. I also describe how their ways of thinking are situated in, and supported by, broader mindsets about the nature of privacy, property, and participation in digital life. Messages from adults figure in here; I draw on youths' reports of the messages they hear from adults about the Internet in addition to direct data from interviews with parents, teachers, and other educators. The portrait I share is particularly attentive to the thinking gaps observed, yet I also point to and describe inspiring, morally, and ethically sensitive modes of thinking engaged in by young people.

Morality and Ethics, As Defined in This Book

When my colleagues and I began studying young people's approaches to online life, we brought to this topic a particular conception of morality and ethics and the distinction between them. My coinvestigator in this project, psychologist Howard Gardner, has often spoken and written about *neighborly morality*, on the one hand, and the *ethics of roles*, on the other. Although he has written about these concepts in a number of places, his book *Truth, Beauty, and Goodness Reframed* provides a particularly focused discussion.[6]

In brief, neighborly morality involves concern for known others, such as family members, friends, neighbors, and other close relations. This kind of morality can take various forms, including conveying respect and compassion, engaging in empathetic perspective taking, and invoking moral principles such as fairness or the Golden Rule, "Do unto others as you would have them do unto you."

Empathy, a central feature of the moral orientation described here, is widely touted these days as a vital moral capacity and, indeed, a virtue.[7] Too little empathy is certainly related to social problems such as bullying.[8] However, Gardner and others contend that goodness in our globally interconnected world requires additional capacities.[9] In a particularly poignant piece, psychologist Paul Bloom makes "the case against empathy," arguing that it is insufficient for the many complex, contemporary issues in which there is no one "identifiable victim" with whom to empathize.[10] Global warming, economic inequality, even genocides in far-flung places fail to attract the necessary attention when we prize "parochial" empathy over a more abstract consideration of how distant people's lives may be affected by the coffee we drink, the clothing we buy, and the cars we drive.

Neighborly morality, or micromorality, as James Rest and colleagues call it, is a useful guide for interactions with direct relations.[11] Yet it falls short or at best has only limited relevance when one is engaging in a larger group, community, public, or even world composed of individuals whom one does not—indeed, cannot—know personally. Here is where Rest's macromorality, an abstract attitude, or an *ethical* disposition is required. Ethical thinking involves considering the effect of one's actions on multiple and distant stakeholders and on the integrity of a larger community.

Related to this, Gardner's concept of the ethics of roles involves reflection on the nature of one's roles (e.g., student, worker, teacher, or citizen) and the associated responsibilities to the larger context (e.g., school, organization, country) in which those roles are situated. Central to ethical thinking is impartiality, or disinterest: the capacity to look beyond one's own interests, feelings, and empathy for close relations in order to make decisions that are in the interests of a larger group, public, or society. For example, a scientist who discovers harmful side effects associated with a cancer drug his company has developed has an ethical responsibility to consider the wider public and not simply the interests of his colleagues and company.

The conceptual distinction between morality and ethics that I've laid out here is utilized throughout the book. When I use the word *moral*, I am referring to a disposition to care, to show empathy, or to engage a principle in one's interactions with a known individual or a small group. When I use the word *ethical*, I am suggesting a more abstract consideration of the effects of one's actions on a wider, often distant, community or public.

This distinction is apt because it highlights an important challenge of the digital age: the comments, memories, and photos we share with our nearest and dearest are also often visible to a wider community of less dear friends and peers and perhaps even strangers. Given the potentially public nature of all online content, the things we say and share on social media sites take on ethical connotations. Although we may wish to take off our student, teacher, or city councilor hat and exchange lighthearted jabs with a friend over Twitter, when our tweets are publicly available, we can't easily escape the expectations and responsibilities associated with these roles.

Moreover, the content we post conveys, either implicitly or explicitly, what is acceptable to communicate in public, thus contributing to norms. The extent to which we are sensitive to this reality, versus freely and obliviously sharing "what's on [our] mind[s]" (as Facebook perpetually asks us to do), is a key area of concern in this book.

Ways of Thinking

In order to study these issues—specifically the degree to which young people consider the moral and especially the ethical dimensions of their online choices—my colleagues and I resolved to focus our attention on the targets of young people's thinking. What are their key considerations when blogging, sharing status updates on Facebook, posting and tagging friends in photos on Flickr, uploading self-made videos to YouTube, contributing to

Wikipedia, downloading music, and strategizing in a massive multiplayer game such as *World of Warcraft*? We sought to understand whose perspectives they consider, whose interests they seek to protect or respect, and how wide their sense of responsibility is on the Web.

The answers to these kinds of questions told us a lot about the extent to which youths' thinking about online situations was largely self-focused, keyed to moral issues, or attuned to broader ethical concerns. Indeed, the three distinct targets implied by these categories—self, known others, and distant others in a larger community—are anchors of the framework of ways of thinking that we used to analyze young people's narratives about online life.[12] Below, I briefly describe these thinking types, with examples of how they appear in relation to online contexts and choices.

The self is the primary focus of what I refer to as *consequence thinking* or *self-focused thinking*. The principal consideration here is the potential consequences for oneself of a particular action.[13] In other words, will I get into trouble if I share my party photos on Instagram? And are the rewards of doing so worth the risks? The rewards associated with a given online action—such as posting a snarky comment on a friend's new Facebook profile picture—may include public markers of social approval, such as "likes" or praising comments. The risks may involve retaliation from the friend, either online or face-to-face. Other online actions, such as piracy or copying text from Wikipedia for a school assignment, may carry more significant risks, ranging from downloading a computer virus to failing a class or even being expelled from school.

Overall, in this way of thinking, positive and negative consequences loom large, and the sense of responsibility is narrowly focused on the self. Although consequence thinking is deeply individualistic, a degree of it is certainly advisable, if not vital. Young people should be attentive to the potential risks and opportunities associated with their choices. However, when the consequences for oneself are the principal basis for online decision making, then the social, moral, and ethical character of the Web suffers.

In line with the discussion of neighborly morality above, the targets of *moral thinking* are known others. When one engages in empathetic perspective taking, conveys respect, or applies the Golden Rule, there is a human face in mind—typically a close friend, a sibling, or another family member. Thus, in relation to online life, moral thinking may involve pausing to consider how a close friend might feel before posting an embarrassing picture of him or her on Twitter. Or it may be deciding, on the basis of moral concerns, to purchase a music CD made by a friend's struggling band rather than burning a copy for free. "Playing nice"—treating other individuals with respect and civility on social networks, in blogs, and in online games—is another example of moral thinking on the Internet.

The key targets of *ethical thinking* include distant, unknown individuals and the integrity of larger communities. Ethical thinking, as we operationalized it in our research, can take three main forms. First, *roles and responsibilities thinking* involves an awareness of one's obligations when considering different courses of action on the Web. Second, *complex perspective taking* includes efforts to consider how one's online actions may affect multiple distant stakeholders.[14] Finally, *community thinking* indicates concern for the potential benefit or harm to a larger community associated with one's online choices.

For example, an ethical or community-oriented approach to cheating in a massive multiplayer game considers the effects of one's gaming strategies on the larger game economy and game experience for all players. Similarly, ethical thinking on YouTube may involve imagining how unknown viewers might respond to, interpret, or misinterpret a video before posting it. Or it could mean considering how different users of Wikipedia (e.g., younger and older people, more and less educated people) might benefit from new information or be harmed by misinformation posted on the collective online encyclopedia.

Finally, attention to the ethics of roles might involve deciding to keep one's opinions about one's employer, students, or patients *off* the Internet. Or it might involve taking care to consider how diverse audiences of known and unknown individuals might respond to one's speech, were it to become public to a wider audience than intended.

Certainly, these three ways of thinking—consequence, moral, and ethical—are not mutually exclusive. Ideally, young people should be considering all three sets of targets—themselves, known others, and wider communities—as they participate in digital environments. However, more often than not, the young people we interviewed were principally, if not exclusively, concerned with their own interests when making decisions online. This might not be surprising. However, it is worthy of critical attention, given the deeply social and interactive nature of online contexts—the fact that the things we do online are potentially boundless or poised to affect countless others.[15]

What We Can Expect of Young People: Insights from Moral Development

These ways of thinking—their appearance, prevalence, and the sophisti-
cation with which they are articulated—are informed by developmental
factors. Moral development theories and studies, including the pioneering
work of Lawrence Kohlberg, and later work by William Damon, James Rest,
and others, lend helpful insights.[16] Kohlberg theorized a general shift over
childhood from an egoistic stance to a concern for close relations and then,
by adolescence, to an awareness of a larger social order.[17] Damon drew on
empirical studies to provide more detail about the workings of moral development. A rudimentary sense of empathy, a foundational element of moral
thinking, can be found even among infants but is more emotionally driven
than cognitively supported at that age. As perspective taking, a cognitive
skill, develops in the toddler and preschool years, so does a more robust
capacity for empathy.[18]

Similarly, principles such as fairness and the Golden Rule are engaged in
the preschool years, though more often with a subjective agenda in mind
(i.e., getting *my* fair share). More objective understandings of such principles
begin to appear among elementary school–age children. As noted, ethical
thinking requires a capacity for abstract thinking, which typically develops
in late childhood or adolescence.[19] Consequently, most teens should have
the capacity to consider how their actions may affect unknown individuals
and a larger community.

In exploring young people's orientations toward the Internet—particularly those of older children and of tweens (which, in our study, we defined
as 10- to 14-year-olds)—it's important be mindful that they are likely to be
adept at moral thinking but that their ethical thinking capacities are still
developing. Adolescents and emerging adults should have stronger ethical
capacities than their younger counterparts, yet for various reasons to be
explored, they might not always exercise them. Related to this, the *capacity*
to think or reason morally or ethically is but one piece of the puzzle—necessary but certainly not sufficient for ethical thinking and action.

Looking beyond the capacity for moral reasoning or judgment, James
Rest and colleagues describe three further components of morality: *moral
sensitivity* (awareness of a moral situation), *moral motivation* (the inclination to prioritize moral considerations over other concerns), and *moral
character* (the capacity to show moral courage, an aspect of identity).[20]

Moral sensitivity precedes the other components; one cannot judge or be motivated to act upon a moral situation if one does not first recognize the situation as moral. Similarly, the literature on thinking dispositions shows that sensitivity to opportunities to engage in careful and critical thinking is more central than the capacity to think at a high level.[21]

In keeping with these ideas, in this book I conceive of moral and ethical thinking as *dispositional*—engendered not only by sheer capacity but also, and perhaps more often, by sensitivity, motivation, and identity. Related to this, my analysis is not about right or wrong choices; indeed, many of the issues that surface in these pages don't lend themselves to clear-cut moral or ethical judgments. Rather, my interest is in where and when young people's thinking includes or lacks moral or ethical sensitivity and an inclination to grapple with the dilemmas.

As I explore young people's thinking about digital spaces in the chapters that follow, I am particularly attentive to the extent to which, and how, youth are morally sensitive (aware of the effects of their actions on known others) and ethically sensitive (cognizant of the distant and wider effects of their actions). I also call attention to obvious failures of sensitivity: the blind spots and disconnects.

Thinking Gaps: Blind Spots and Disconnects

In making sense of the gaps in young people's thinking about online situations, I draw inspiration from behavioral ethics—and specifically the work of Max Bazerman and Ann Tenbrunsel. In their book, *Blind Spots*, the authors distill a large body of empirical research about *bounded ethicality*, or the common, unconscious tendency to be more attentive to and "favor our own self-interest at the expense of the interests of others."[22] Blind spots are often present regardless of the strength of one's moral and ethical values and one's self-conception as a good person.

For example, the authors describe a mother who is considering not vaccinating her children because of an alleged link between vaccinations and autism. In her focus on the health and well-being of her own children, the mother fails to consider the possible negative effects of nonvaccination on her children's playmates and the larger public. This example serves to illustrate not only bounded ethicality but also *ethical fading*, in which the ethical dimensions of a situation or problem fade from view as other concerns are brought to the foreground.[23]

In young people's narratives about online life, we observed frequent moral and ethical blind spots. When deciding whether to share one's weekend pictures on Facebook, to cheat in a massive multiplayer game, or to copy text from Wikipedia into a research paper, youth were often blind to the moral and ethical features of these decisions. Young people's decision making about such issues was certainly not thoughtless. However, the thinking in which they engaged was often deeply self-focused—that is, what might *I* gain or lose from a given choice?

In some cases, the ethical blind spots observed were entangled with blind spots about the qualities of digital content and context. For instance, many youths appeared to lose sight (even if only temporarily) of the public nature of online contexts as well as the ease of copying and sharing information to a larger audience than intended. In these cases, technical blind spots thus contributed to, and even compounded, the ethical ones.

Ethical blind spots are somewhat distant relatives of what I refer to as *disconnects*. Whereas blind spots are unconscious, naive, and unintentional, disconnects are quite conscious, even mindful. A disconnect occurs when the moral or ethical dimensions of a situation are recognized and considered but then summarily dismissed in favor of self-focused interests. For instance, one young woman told us about some musician friends who were losing money because people were downloading their music illegally rather than purchasing it. Although she acknowledged their struggles, she then conveyed indifference to them: "So it's like, they're losing money. But I don't know. I kind of don't care at the same time."

Revisiting the three cases described at the beginning of this chapter, we can perceive both blind spots and disconnects. Whether or not we believe Dharun Ravi, who used a webcam to spy on his roommate, his statements suggest that he was simply not considering—that is, he was blind to—the potential harm of his actions. Ravi also appeared not to think about the public nature of his tweets.

Helen Hegemann, the young German writer, adopted a model of creativity that was blind to the effects on other writers whose words she appropriated. However, we can also detect a mindful disconnect on her part, at least after she was accused of plagiarism. Although she apologized, she also defended her creative approach.

The New York City police officers who vented on Facebook about their duties, and about the people they were charged with protecting and serving, were blind to the ethical responsibilities associated with their professional roles—and, related to this, to the public nature of the context in which they were complaining. The ease with which the Facebook content could be copied—as it was before the page was deleted—also escaped the participants' attention. At once, the egregiously hateful and racist nature of some comments—such as "It's not racist if it's true"—stand as evidence of mindful disconnects at work.

Behavioral ethicists like Bazerman and Tenbrunsel show that bounded ethicality, ethical fading, and other phenomena that contribute to blind spots are widespread and manifest in diverse spheres of life. Mindful disconnects—conscious decisions to pursue one's own agenda despite the potential negative effects on others—are prevalent to an unfortunate degree, too. Given the topic of this book, and the technical blind spots referred to above, it is critical to engage the question of how digitally mediated modes of communication may coincide with, and even facilitate, blind spots and disconnects, as well as more prosocial thinking dispositions.

How Being Digital Matters

It is undeniable that digital media have changed our lives in myriad ways. As Nicholas Negroponte described in *Being Digital*, the shift from the physical to the digital, from atoms to bits as dominant carriers of information and other content, has been monumental.[24] Digital technologies have paved the way for newer, faster, and arguably richer ways to share content and connect with one another than we had at our disposal even just 20 years ago.

The implications of the digital revolution for adolescent development, for learning, for creativity and innovation, for exposure to diverse perspectives, and for democratic participation, among other outcomes, are widely conjectured and beginning to be understood. Developmental psychologists, including Katie Davis, Kaveri Subrahmanyam, and Patti Valkenburg, have found that online communication can support identity and intimacy development; yet other factors, such as the quality of a youth's friendships and parental relationships, remain important contributors to positive developmental outcomes.[25]

Turning to the broader implications of the web, optimists such as Clay Shirky place considerable stock in the capacity for collaboration and collective action made possible by the Internet. Similarly, Mimi Ito and colleagues have unearthed the great learning potentials of informal, interest-based online communities. Finally, Clive Thompson argues that the Internet elevates human intelligence.[26]

Yet pessimists, including thinkers such as Nicholas Carr, Jaron Lanier, and Sherry Turkle, have detailed more troubling consequences of our increasingly digital lives on our attention, thinking, identities, and relationships. As Carr points out, just as books and clocks transformed our thinking, digital technologies are also "intellectual technologies"; they change how we think and what we think *about*; his concern is that our thinking is frequently scattered and shallow. Jaron Lanier carries this idea further, arguing that the design of digital technologies locks in particular modes of thinking and action, with implications for our sense of humanity.[27]

Howard Gardner and Katie Davis argue that even though digital media can enhance our lives in myriad ways, excessive dependence on apps can undercut the development of healthy identities, relationships with others, and our capacities for creativity. Finally, media theorist Roger Silverstone tackled the moral and ethical significance of the digital age more directly, arguing that the distance between ourselves and others is standardized online; neighbors and strangers are at an equal distance from us, which alters and widens our spheres of responsibility.[28]

Both optimistic and skeptical accounts allude to a core set of qualities and affordances that mark digital technologies and distinguish them from prior media forms. First, there is the *interactive* or *participatory* quality of the Internet, represented by the concept of Web 2.0. Henry Jenkins lauds the "participatory cultures," or interest-oriented communities, that have flourished via the Internet.[29]

Indeed, the capacity to collaborate and participate in public, civic, and political life—through online dialogue, organizing, production, and circulation of content—is arguably unprecedented.[30] This quality may be particularly significant for many young people today, who enter and actively take part in the public sphere at earlier ages than in the past. The openness of the Internet is not without its drawbacks, however; in allowing any and all voices, hateful ideas can circulate as often as compassionate ones.

The participatory nature of the Web is intensified by another quality: *scalability*, the potential for online content to be shared with a wide, even global, public. Indeed, as danah boyd describes, scalability, or the possibility of unintended audiences, is one of four unique properties of networked publics that young people must negotiate on social network sites.[31] The other three qualities—*persistence, replicability*, and *searchability*—are focused more narrowly on the nature of digital content. In other words, digital content sticks: it is easily copied, pasted, forwarded, uploaded, and downloaded—and it is searchable. Therefore, the things you choose to share on Facebook or Tumblr may haunt you, and the people featured and tagged in your photos or comments, indefinitely.

Constant connectivity, or the opportunity to be continuously in touch with others via mobile phones and other devices, may help us maintain our relationships, especially with distant friends and family.[32] At the same time, Sherry Turkle and others argue, being "always on" may weaken our relationships, since our interactions are reduced to text messages and our face-to-face time is often interrupted, our attention pulled away by the lure of a notification from our phones. Douglas Rushkoff maintains that we are trapped in a perpetual "now," a "present shock."[33]

Moreover, being tethered to one another digitally can diminish, if not erase, the alone time required to develop a sense of autonomy, a key marker of a healthy identity and a precondition for ethical thinking.[34] Constant connectivity can also permit relentless, around-the-clock bullying. In terms of how we speak to one another online, the *asynchronous* and *text-dominant* qualities of much Web-based communication can permit time to choose our words carefully, reflect, and edit before conveying our thoughts.[35] Yet these same qualities can pose problems because the lack of tone leaves status updates, tweets, and comments subject to misinterpretation.

One of the most salient qualities of digital communication in relation to the focus of this book is the *distance* that our phones, tablets, and computers place between us. When we communicate largely by screen, asynchronously, using text, we may feel quite removed from the individuals to whom our messages and content are directed; the other, incidental audiences for what we share may not even occur to us. Another way to put it is that we interact at arm's length when we text, instant-message, or tweet.

Silverstone wrote at length about the distant quality of digital life, observing that "the mediated face makes no demands on us, because we have the power to switch it off and to withdraw." Given this power to withdraw, he argued, "an ethics for cyberspace must ... be able to encompass distance as a crucial component of the moral life, and it must address the problem of how we can behave responsibly in our dealings with mediated others."[36]

Related to the arm's length quality of online communication is what John Suler called the "online disinhibition effect," in which some "people say and do things in cyberspace that they wouldn't ordinarily say and do in the face-to-face world."[37] Suler described how online disinhibition can be benign and even a positive mode of identity exploration. But disinhibition can also take toxic forms, such as flaming, trolling, and hate speech. In exploring the disinhibition effect, Suler points to *anonymity* as a contributor to this phenomenon.

Opportunities for anonymity may be diminishing, however. Some social media sites, such as Facebook, require the use of real names, and this practice is being adopted by some news sites as a way of promoting more civil discourse in commenting.[38] Yet other online contexts—such as Reddit, Twitter, and Tumblr—continue to offer mechanisms, even if not foolproof ones, for participating anonymously.

The increasingly blurred boundaries between our online interactions and our offline lives can heighten our moral and ethical sensitivity, thus weakening the disinhibition effect and perhaps closing the distance between what we do and its effects on others. However, we may be less morally and ethically concerned when we interact anonymously and with people whom we don't know offline. Moreover, our propensities for multitasking while online may result in limited time to reflect about online exchanges even with intimates. Empirical studies strongly suggest that cognitive overload impairs ethical decision making.[39]

Consequently, when shifting among social media sites, our email inboxes, text messages, and work-related documents, we may be less morally and ethically sensitive, or even blind, to the potential effects on others of what we say and do. As Sherry Turkle puts it, "As we communicate in ways that ask for almost instantaneous responses, we don't allow the space to consider complicated problems."[40]

The unique qualities that characterize digital media and the Internet are therefore double-edged, presenting opportunities as well as challenges for learning and creativity, for democracy, and for our relationships. They have mixed moral and ethical potentials, too. Qualities such as interactivity, persistence, replicability, searchability, and scalability in particular raise the stakes of our activities, turning previously ordinary practices (such as sharing photos with friends) into morally and ethically loaded ones.

Indeed, whether or not we acknowledge it, our routine online practices often constitute moral and ethical *dilemmas*. Alertness to the dilemmas and the implications inherent in many of our online choices seems vital. However, other qualities of online life may dull our sensitivity to these issues. The lack of tone in text-based communications, the opportunity for anonymity, and the general arm's length quality of our interactions puts others at a distance. Finally, certain habits of connectivity—the propensity to be constantly connected and to multitask—may undercut the inclination to reflect and edit before clicking Send or Share.

Given these qualities of digital life and our related habits, blind spots and disconnects on the part of both young people and adults may be expected. When operating at a distance, thinking about and attempting to grasp the effects of our choices on others requires cognitive capacity and effort as well as a disposition to be sensitive to moral and ethical concerns in general. Unfortunately, recent data about the moral and ethical commitments of both young people and adults paint a troubling picture.

Blind Spots and Disconnects in the Broader Culture

At least in the United States, young people today are growing up not just in a digital world but in a world in which individualism—an emphasis on responsibility for oneself and personal success—endures as a cherished value.[41] High-profile ethical lapses on the part of leaders in sectors ranging from financial services to government to higher education suggest a cultural emphasis on profits and self-advancement above social responsibility. Certainly there are positive role models, counterforces, and even movements to direct young people's attention and lives toward civic and community concerns—and there are impressive examples of youths who exhibit a strong sense of purpose about issues in the wider world. Nevertheless, recent studies also document an enduring, if not growing, empathy gap and general preoccupation with the self among many young people.[42]

Psychologist Jean Twenge's body of work, including her provocatively titled books, *Generation Me* and *The Narcissism Epidemic*, suggests that individualistic personality traits have increased among young Americans in the last several decades. Sara Konrath's studies on the extent of self-focused and other-focused dispositions among American college students have revealed recent declines in empathetic concern and perspective taking. Although there may be signs of a reversal of some of these trends, individualistic attitudes are still pervasive to a troubling degree.[43]

Related to this, we also see evidence of widespread, and perhaps growing, trends in unethical conduct. In the book *Making Good*, Wendy Fischman and colleagues reveal that many young people are willing to cheat or otherwise cut corners to get ahead of or keep up with their peers in school and at work. Even though these young people had strong ethical beliefs and values, they decided that they simply couldn't afford to be ethical until they had succeeded.[44] Recent cases of cheating at highly selective high schools and colleges reveal that the problem is indeed widespread, even among the best and the brightest. Other writers argue that a deeper "cheating culture" is endemic in the United States and beyond.[45]

Finally, we find powerful evidence of moral and ethical blind spots in a large number of young people, as documented in Christian Smith and colleagues' recent book, *Lost in Transition*. In a longitudinal study that included surveys and interviews with "emerging adults" (ages 18–23) in the United States, Smith's research team found an unsettling degree of moral and ethical blindness. When the researchers asked the youths to tell them about a moral dilemma they had recently grappled with, two-thirds were unable to identify a problem that was objectively moral or ethical in nature.

Instead, they responded with practical or personal dilemmas, such as whether to rent an apartment that was just beyond their means. The authors concluded that "emerging adults do not have a good handle on what makes something a *moral* issue or what the specifically *moral* dimensions of such situations are. The idea of distinctively moral goods and bads, rights and wrongs, is not engaged. What comes to the fore instead are straightforwardly practical, utilitarian, financial, and psychological dilemmas."[46]

Furthermore, when Smith's team probed in more explicit ways about moral issues, most young people responded with *moral individualism*: the belief that what is right or wrong is in the eyes of the beholder. In seeking to explain the gaps they observed, Smith and his colleagues don't lay the blame on the young people themselves, either as individuals or as a generation. Rather, they point to larger sociological forces as well as the failure of adults to provide young people with "intellectual tools" and other supports for thinking about and leading a moral life.

These data points from other research provide an important backdrop to the focus of this book: the moral and ethical sensibilities young people bring, or fail to bring, to their participation on the Internet. The backdrop suggests the presence of both an empathy gap and an ethics gap. So it's not surprising that moral and ethical insensitivity manifest online, too. However, the forms these gaps take are distinct, intertwined as they are with the unique qualities and affordances of digital contexts and our related connectivity habits. The reality is that constant connectivity—the expectation that one will always be in reach—is increasingly a "social fact."[47] Youth in particular feel the weight of this expectation, immersed as they are in a life stage in which connection with peers feels as essential as food and water. The account I give in this book amounts to a portrait of young people's habits of mind as they go about their habits of connectivity.

The Research

The data that inform this book were collected as part of the Good Play Project, a six-year research and educational initiative funded by the John D. and Catherine T. MacArthur Foundation. Howard Gardner and I codirected the initiative at Project Zero, a research center at the Harvard Graduate School of Education. Our research team consisted of 14 researchers across three phases of research, which we carried out between 2008 and 2012. Our studies began with a focus on teens and young adults (ages 15–25). We then turned to a study of tweens (ages 10–14) and key adults in tweens' lives, including parents and teachers. In our last phase, we conducted a small study of teens involved in "digital citizenship" activities, such as efforts to address online cruelty and create socially positive communities on the Web. In total, we talked with 103 young people and 40 adults. Further details about our study and the participants can be found in the appendix. Here, I give a brief sketch of the research, setting the stage for the data I share in the rest of the book.

When we set out to study this problem space, we sought to speak with youths who spend a significant amount of time online and who engage in different kinds of activities, including blogging, content creation, gaming, and use of social network sites. The young people with whom we spoke were diverse in terms of sex, race, ethnicity, and socioeconomic background. This diversity was an important feature of our study—we wanted to hear from youths who may engage with and experience the Web in different ways. However, we did not seek to compare the thinking or the moral and ethical sensitivity of the youths by demographic characteristics. The small size of our sample, among other limitations, would make any claims—particularly about racial, ethnic, and class differences—problematic.

Our methodological approach was primarily qualitative. Using semistructured protocols, we conducted in-depth interviews with each participant. Specifically, a member of our research team sat down face-to-face with nearly every young person, twice, for one to two hours each sitting.[48] We designed the interviews with open-ended questions aimed at eliciting rich and authentic narratives about participants' online lives—including details about the online spaces in which they most frequently engaged and accounts of the individuals (including parents, siblings, peers, and online-only friends) who were poised to support their online activities and choices.

In the interviews, we explored five ethically tinged themes, including online identity, credibility, privacy, property, and participation.[49] We also asked broader, open-ended questions that invited the youths to share their perceptions of the opportunities and risks of digital life. Finally, we shared hypothetical scenarios about different online topics with the participants, engaging them in discussion of how they might respond and about any similar experiences they may have had. Three of the scenarios shared with our study participants are featured in this book.

Crucially, we sought to create a natural, positive rapport with the young people. This meant putting them at ease about the confidential nature of our study and our desire to understand the nature of their experiences with and their perspectives on digital life. Although our particular interest was in the moral and ethical dimensions of online situations, we never used those words; instead, we asked them about norms in online spaces, positive online connections, notions of online community, any troubling situations they had observed, and others areas of concern.

When we perceived apprehension about different lines of inquiry, we made statements to the effect that certain controversial issues—such as privacy and music downloading—are approached and managed in different ways by young people and adults alike, that we weren't seeking to judge their choices, and that above all, we wanted to understand their thinking. We often reiterated the message that we weren't looking for a correct answer but just wanted to hear their points of view. Our research team, largely composed of digitally savvy young people, played a key role in creating a safe space for the youths to share their stories.[50]

Our interviews yielded rich and detailed narratives about the young people's online worlds—the exciting, engaging, and inspiring aspects as well as the more troubling situations and points of struggle. As I illustrate in the thematic chapters, the interviews revealed disconnects and blind spots but also concerted and impressive efforts on the part of some youths to negotiate the complex moral and ethical quandaries posed by the Web.

A final comment about the research: in a relatively short period, the digital world has changed our lives immeasurably, and it is likely to continue to do so. Anyone researching this rapidly changing area is studying a moving target. The rigor required to collect and look closely at data—especially qualitative data—about anything digital is arguably at odds with the pace of change underway.

The empirical studies that inform this book were conducted between 2008 and 2012. During that time alone, we observed changes in the popularity of certain social media sites: the growing popularity of Facebook over MySpace, for instance. We also witnessed the development of new features and policies that impinge on our sense of privacy, that provide new venues for access to content, and that limit opportunities for anonymity, among other changes. As you are reading this book, you may wonder about the applicability of the data to the moment in which you are living. I wonder about that, too. At the same time, I feel convinced that the qualities of online life I discussed above—the persistence and scalability of digital content, constant connectivity, and so on—are defining features of the online experience, regardless of the comings and goings of particular platforms.

This is not to say that we won't develop good mechanisms for managing the challenging aspects of these qualities or that further qualities won't emerge down the road. However, in many respects, the sea change has already happened. The data I draw on in this book represent youth, and adults, at a particular moment in time *after* that sea change. I believe that their ways of thinking reveal fundamental and lasting insights about the opportunities and challenges of being digital for our moral and ethical sensibilities.

What Follows

In the chapters that follow, I explore young people's narratives about their experiences and choices in online contexts, including social network sites, blogs, content-sharing sites, and gaming communities. My attention is focused on the ways of thinking that youth exhibit—ranging from morally and ethically sensitive to self-focused, ethically blind, and disconnected—in relation to archetypal dilemmas of online privacy, property, and participation. I begin each chapter with a detailed digital dilemma and describe further dilemmas related to the topic. I then describe our findings about young people's thinking, tracing them to broader, socially and culturally supported mindsets about the topics at hand.

In chapter 2, I describe young people's approaches to privacy on the Web. I describe how self-focused, consequence-oriented thinking about privacy on the Internet often goes hand in hand with a broader mindset that privacy is "in your hands," or under the control of the individual. When moral and, more rarely, ethical stances toward online privacy appear, they do so in the context of a mindset that recognizes privacy as a social matter, to be negotiated with one's online and offline ties. Finally, the belief that privacy is ultimately forsaken on the Web emerges as well; among some youths, this mindset supports an "anything goes" attitude that coincides with privacy invasions.

In chapter 3, I explore young people's approaches to property issues on the Web. I detail how, in certain contexts, young people invoke conceptions of ownership and authorship in which a single creator should retain rights to his or her product and in which others' use of the content without credit, permission, or payment amounts to copying or stealing. I call this a "what's theirs is theirs" mindset and describe its close ally, "what's mine is mine." I also share the thinking of young people who adopt a "free for all" mindset that suggests that cultural content should be widely accessible for public consumption and use.

In chapter 4, I address the broad theme of participation, focusing my attention on young people's mindsets about cheating in games and negative speech in online contexts such as social networks, blogs, and forums. I describe evidence of a "play nice" mindset among youth, which emphasizes fairness and the feelings of others and a rarer "it's a community" mindset that is sensitive to the broader, ethical implications of one's online choices.

I explore how these mindsets are at odds with a more dismissive "it's just the Internet" stance, in which online content and actions are often treated as "just a joke."

In each of the thematic chapters, I also share data on the messages about online privacy, property, and speech that young people hear from adults in their lives, including parents, teachers, coaches, and employers. I consider how these messages, along with developmental, social, and cultural factors, contribute to the more troubling mindsets, blind spots, and disconnects that young people adopt in relation to the Internet.

In the conclusion, chapter 5, I consider how we might correct the blind spots, reconnect the disconnects, and confront the mindsets that support a digital ethics gap. I describe a vision of conscientious connectivity aimed at addressing the ethics gap. I discuss the roles that parents, peers, educators, and technology companies might play in cultivating conscientious connectivity. I also call attention to, and draw inspiration from, inspiring efforts of young people who seek to make the Internet a kinder, more respectful, and ethical place.

What This Book Is—and Is Not—About: My Biases and Blind Spots

A key acknowledgment is in order at this juncture. As you may realize by now, the story I tell in these pages is more of a "glass half empty" story. The concerns I share and the gaps I point out are likely to be challenged by digital optimists, most of whose work I respect, admire, and think is an equally important piece of the puzzle of how the digital world is changing all of us, young and old. I do share with the optimists an excitement and a sense of hope about the learning, civic, social, and political potentials of the Internet.

At the same time, I harbor real concerns about the local and global consequences, often hidden, of the uncivil, cruel, and harmful conduct that is common, if not routine, in some online communities. I worry that such conduct discourages participation, thus undercutting one of the central promises of the Internet. I also worry about the general lack of attention to moral and ethical concerns on the Internet, compared with the emphasis on personal safety issues.

You may also detect some blind spots in my discussion of the moral and ethical dilemmas associated with digital life. In the substantive chapters,

I don't attend, at length, to the policies and practices of social media and other technology companies like Facebook, Google, and Twitter. Nor do I address the ethical dimensions of targeted advertising and government surveillance practices that diminish privacy. These omissions are not meant to suggest that the technologies these entities design and the policies they make are not ethically loaded.[51] Indeed, their decisions lay the groundwork for the ways in which we engage with one another, and with content, online.

Nonetheless, my focus in this book is on the themes that emerged as most salient to, and under the alleged control of, young people. In other words, my emphasis is on horizontal (peer-to-peer, user-to-user) as opposed to vertical (user–to–social media company) ethical issues, especially in relation to privacy and participation.[52] In spotlighting young people's stances on privacy, property, and participation, I thus mention these entities only to the extent that the youths spoke about them. However, in the concluding chapter, I do consider how social media companies might play a more proactive role in addressing the ethics gap documented in this book.

2   Privacy

Tagged: Found Out on Facebook

Imagine you are a varsity athlete at your college. Your team has a policy that prohibits going to a party before a game. This is also a dry policy for team members, age 21 and older, who drink alcohol. Your friends, who are not on the team, convince you to go to this week's party, which is the night before a big playoff game. They tell you that no one, and certainly not your coach or your teammates, will know you were there.

The next day, when you sign into your Facebook account, you see that one of your friends has posted some public photos of the party and has tagged you in 10 photos. You are concerned that your coach, who is a Facebook friend with you, will see the photos and bench you for the big game. What would you do?

You may not be a college athlete, subject to rules against parties and alcohol—or someone who would ever consider breaking such rules. Even so, you may have been in a comparable situation yourself. Perhaps you declined an invitation to a friend's party, telling him you needed a quiet night at home. Yet hours later, you got a second wind and were convinced by other friends to go out. Someone snapped a photo, uploaded it to Facebook, and indicated the location and time using the check-in feature.

When your friend the party host checks his Facebook news feed, there you are—not having a quiet night at home at all. In the digital age, it's easy to imagine a host of scenarios in which social media reveal your activities to unintended audiences. Below, I present snapshots of how youth think about and manage this reality and the extent to which they consider the moral and ethical dimensions of privacy and publicity in a digital age. But first imagine you found yourself in the college athlete situation. How might you think about it, and what would you do?

Consider your options. You could untag yourself from the photos, which halts the "so-and-so was tagged in 'the best party ever' photos" story from appearing in the news feeds of your Facebook friends, including your coach and your teammates. Nevertheless, even though you are now untagged, your coach and your teammates may be friends with the photographer or other tagged people and may notice you in the pictures anyway. Given the probability of being exposed in this way, perhaps your safest bet is to ask your friend to remove from Facebook all the party photos that include you. Your friend could balk at the suggestion, citing her right to post whatever she sees fit. After all, you chose to ignore the rules and attend the party, so you should face up to the consequences. Perhaps you're now wondering whether you can access your friend's account somehow and delete the photos yourself.

Notably, these courses of action assume that your primary goal is to hide, if not destroy, any evidence of your breach. It may be understandable to be thinking about (and perhaps even seeking to mitigate) potential undesirable consequences to yourself. But what are some other ways to think about this dilemma?

You could consider the scenario from the perspectives of your coach and your teammates. How would they feel about your violation? You might reflect on the principles behind the rules—the most salient being the need to be well-rested and ready to play, especially for a big playoff game. Your coach and your teammates might feel let down and perceive your actions as putting your social life above your commitment to the team. They might lose trust in you and seek to have you benched for the big game—or worse, kicked off the team.

This set of considerations focuses on the effect of your breach on people whom, presumably, you know fairly well and perhaps even care about. Finally, you could reflect on the more distant effects of your actions. You might ask yourself about the messages your now-public breach convey to other student athletes whom you don't know, or even the wider community of students at your college.

"Untag Me!": Teens and Young Adults Respond

Underlying these different courses of action are three distinct targets of thinking: the self, known others, and a distant and larger community. We might expect, or at least hope, that all three types of targets are considered when one confronts such a dilemma. However, when we presented this dilemma to teens and young adults, they typically framed their responses around one key target: themselves.

Nineteen-year-old Justine's response was emblematic of the self-focused approach: "I'd probably untag the pictures ... to save my own butt." Nearly 80 percent of the teens and young adults to whom we presented this scenario sought to avoid "getting into trouble" at all costs. These youth were largely unconcerned that their own (hypothetical) actions, attending the party in violation of a rule, had landed them in this undesirable situation in the first place.

Although this was presented as a hypothetical scenario, its key features were very familiar to the youths. One college student spoke about perpetually "dodging cameras" at parties in order to avoid being tagged online, and many youths expressed anxiety about managing the Internet afterlives of their offline activities.[1] One teen, Violet, framed the hypothetical situation as unfair to her: "I would plead and ask, 'Hey, can you untag those, take them off, something? I don't care, but just do something, because that is really unfair to me.'... My first reaction would be getting myself to be able to play the game. That would be my first concern." Above all, Violet saw herself as an innocent victim in the scenario.

The prevalence of the self-focused, consequence-oriented approach suggests a blindness on the part of many teens and young adults to the moral and ethical dimensions of their offline choices—a blind spot with high stakes, given the increasingly blurred boundaries between offline and online life. Consistent with this notion, only three youths commented that they never would have broken the team policy and attended the party in the first place. So even though all the youths were keenly aware that their offline actions were potentially public to unintended audiences, their typical response was to attempt to control the audiences rather than to reconsider their conduct.

Furthermore, some indicated that managing this reality sometimes necessitates lying about one's actions. When Justine was asked if she would consider talking to her teammates or her coach, she said, "Probably. I mean excuses aren't too hard to come up with, you know. 'Oh, I had to, I was DD [designated driver],' ... I would [say], 'Look, I really didn't want to go, but my friends were going to drive drunk; I couldn't let them do that.'" Justine's self-preservationist approach goes beyond simply untagging the photos to concocting a story that makes her actions appear acceptable, even socially responsible.

However, not all the youths with whom we spoke completely disregarded the moral and ethical features of this situation. When prompted by the interviewer, 32 percent of the teens and young adults with whom we shared this scenario acknowledged a responsibility to the team. Michelle, age 17, reflected, "I would let them down if I was to get caught. I could've been a good player, essential to the team, and [they might feel] like, 'All right, so you're getting benched, and we have to play this game by ourselves, and we need your help.' So I would think about them. But not as much as I would think about myself, like getting in trouble and other leading consequences." Michelle takes the perspectives of her teammates, wondering how her actions and their likely consequences will harm the team's chances of winning the game. Yet she also says that her primary concern would be avoiding negative consequences for herself.

Sixteen percent of the teens and young adults were primarily moral thinkers about this scenario—they were most concerned with the effects of their actions on their close relations. Keith, age 23, was one of the few respondents who said that he never would have broken the rule. He added, "[I'd be] disappointing the coach and disappointing my team.... I'm not taking their policy seriously, I'm not taking the team seriously, and I'm not going to perform my best because I was out partying the night before a big game. Then that kind of sucks for everybody else who put in their time, practiced hard, and didn't go out and party and might not even get to play and be on the bench." Keith is keenly attuned to the purpose of the policy and the potential negative effects of his breach for the team.

Only one teen perceived the dilemma in a broader way, hinting at the ways in which conduct that is publicized online sets norms. Thomas, age 18, said, "I would apologize for being irresponsible. And also, if I'm an upperclassman, say how I'm not setting a good example." In recognizing that his conduct can send a bad message to a wider community of students, Thomas was the only respondent who was attuned to its ethical dimensions.

Below, I consider related data about youth's lived experiences with and approaches to online privacy issues. First, I describe a range of privacy dilemmas—personal, moral, and ethical—that are heightened by the technologies at our disposal and our habits of connectivity in the digital age.

I then turn to data about the extent to which youth care about privacy issues and their motives for sharing online. These data set the stage for a discussion of three distinct mindsets about privacy that appeared, to various degrees, in our interviews with youth: privacy as social, privacy as "in your hands," and privacy as forsaken online. I discuss how these mindsets are marked by different levels of sensitivity to the moral and ethical dimensions of privacy. Finally, I discuss how messages from adults may contribute to the dominance of certain mindsets and explore some related moral or ethical disconnects and blind spots.

Privacy and Publicity in a Digital Age: The Dilemmas

The hypothetical but realistic tagged scenario calls attention to an important social fact of the digital age: many of the routine *offline* choices we make are now potentially publicized to a wider audience, even of friends, than we intended. None of us are exempt from this social fact—people who elect not to join online social networks are often unconsenting participants on Facebook, YouTube, and the like, since both well-intentioned and malintentioned users share photos, videos, and comments featuring these nonusers.

This reality poses dilemmas for all of us that apply not only to situations involving explicit rule violations, as in the college athlete scenario, but to our conduct in general. In June 2011, a New York subway commuter was recorded by an onlooker as she rudely chastised a conductor. A video was posted on YouTube, and soon the woman was publicly identified and mocked for her tirade.[2] A colleague recently told me a story about a conflict that ensued between friends after a video of a child's birthday party was posted on Facebook. While the focus of the video was the celebration—and the intent in posting it was to share it with distant family members—the video also contained, in the background, a "regrettable parenting moment" (a harsh scolding) between a mother and a child in attendance. When the video was posted, the mother felt publicly embarrassed and asked that the video be taken down, but the friends refused, and the friendship ultimately ended over the affair.

At one point or another, most of us have made a poor decision, disrespected another person, or said things we've regretted. For those of us who grew up before the digital revolution, those missteps are likely forgotten—or exist only in our own fuzzy memories or in the memories of direct witnesses. Today it's a whole different ball game. The potential exists for our mistakes to live on, and even outlive us, casting an eternal shadow over our reputations. This reality places enormous pressure on us to avoid missteps.

It's nearly inevitable, though, that missteps will be taken, especially by young people who are exploring and developing their identities and often taking age-appropriate risks. When missteps are shared online, as they increasingly are, we have a dilemma on our hands. We can try, perhaps in vain, to bury the evidence. Or we can face up to our conduct and attend to any harm with as much humility and integrity as possible.

Indeed, whether we are willing or reluctant citizens of the digital world, we face a series of dilemmas. In addition to the dilemmas of how we conduct ourselves and respond to public exposure by others online, we confront personal dilemmas about how much of our own lives to share online: our biographical information, phone numbers, location at any given time, relationship status, political leanings, and so on. An overwhelming amount of attention—in the media, in education, and in scholarship—is focused on this personal risk aspect of privacy: how online content may negatively affect our safety and reputations.

In many ways, this emphasis is understandable, given the properties of digital content highlighted by danah boyd and others—the fact that content persists and is replicable, searchable, and potentially shareable with unintended audiences.[3] As Jeffrey Rosen aptly put it, "The Web means the end of forgetting."[4] Digital technologies significantly reduce our capacity to keep aspects of our identities separate and confined to the relevant audience. The concern is particularly salient for children and adolescents who, for various reasons to be explored below, may not always be alert to the range of potential audiences for their online conduct.

It would be a mistake, however, to consider this problem space only from the perspective of personal risk. After all, once our conduct is visible to others in public networks, it sets an example. Moreover, while the star of a troubling scenario is the person appearing in the incriminating photo or video, the other key player is the one behind the camera and screen. That is, online privacy mishaps involve an individual who made a regrettable choice *and* the person who recorded it and subsequently shared it with a wide audience. Sometimes we are the star; sometimes we are the producer. (Of course, when we develop a Twitter or LinkedIn profile, we are both producer and star.)

So even as we face unsettling personal dilemmas about privacy, the deeply social nature of online social networks suggests that these are moral and ethical dilemmas, too. As we share pictures of our hikes, beach vacations, and nightclub outings, we are also often sharing images of our friends, family members, and other people in the background—the "costars" and "extras" in the ongoing Facebook or Instagram movie of our lives. We can tag friends in our status updates or check-ins at restaurants and museums whether or not they're actually with us. Ideally, our alertness to the privacy and digital footprints of others should happen alongside the concern for our own privacy. But does it?

Moral and ethical dilemmas also arise in our roles as audiences for online content. Sometimes we are relatively passive observers, scanning our Twitter and Tumblr feeds for amusing photos and friend updates. At other times, though, we are active and strategic consumers of online content, Googling new acquaintances, old classmates, and even potential business partners or clients.

Moral and ethical questions arise as we become privy to others' digital trails, whether we do so intentionally or quite incidentally. We may notice sensitive information about a colleague being shared by a mutual friend on a social network. Or we may be tempted to look to an Internet search engine when we want to know whether a prospective employee has a reputable or sordid past. We then face dilemmas of how to assess and use the information we discover. Do we take what we find at face value, treat it as truth and possibly as grounds for judging someone unfit for a job, a date, or friendship? Or do we take online content with a grain of salt and perhaps request more information or an explanation so that we may understand and, if appropriate, excuse or forgive?

Careful attention must be paid to the approaches that both youth and adults are taking to the thorny privacy dilemmas unfolding in this evolving landscape. In presenting the tagged scenario to the participants in our study, we sought to understand what sense of responsibility is triggered, and to whom, when an action—in this case, attending a party in violation of a school team policy—is made public online. The intention was to explore to what extent an online revelation provokes moral regret as well as larger ethical considerations. What we observed was relatively little moral regret and almost no ethical thinking. Instead, we found largely self-focused approaches that prescribed untagging or removing incriminating

photos from public view and, among a few young people, a willingness to
lie in order to avoid getting caught.

In addition to presenting the youths with hypothetical scenarios, we
also spoke with them about their lived digital experiences, the privacy
approaches they adopt, and the considerations that guide their choices.
We found that their personal narratives about online privacy—and their
approaches to a range of online privacy dilemmas—are also deeply self-
focused and, at times, contain striking ethical disconnects and blind spots.

Privacy Matters: Youth Perspectives

If we are to believe popular media accounts and the complaints of many
parents and teachers, young people today are either oblivious to the audiences for their digital footprints or see privacy as a relic of a bygone era and
resign themselves to leading very public lives. Set against our data—and
a growing body of other research—these assertions look very much like
myths, or at least misinterpretations, of young people's sharing practices on
social media sites and in other "networked publics."[5]

When tweens, teens, and young adults spoke with us about privacy in
the digital age, several themes came vividly to the fore. First, we observed
that they valued privacy, both online and offline. They also thought about
it in largely conventional ways. In their accounts, privacy is about controlling content about yourself and the audiences for that content. Madeline,
age 21, said, "Privacy, to me, means that people I don't know can't find out
where I am. I don't want people that I don't know knowing where I am or
what I'm doing." To 19-year-old Serena, privacy means, more succinctly,
that "people that you want to see your stuff can see your stuff but not
everybody." These conceptions of privacy hardly seem new; rather, they
align with the views of many older adults.

The second theme that stood out is the degree to which the youths were
sensitive to personal privacy risks online and thus took measures to protect their information and content. So even while their notions of privacy
were conventional, the youths understood that online contexts strain these
notions. Regardless of age, most argued that they have more privacy offline
than they do online. Eleven-year-old Anthony said it was more difficult to
create privacy online "because other people, if they go against you and if
they were your friends one time … they could have took [sic] all that information to embarrass you online and let everyone who is online know. And

then everyone at school, or anywhere, would be laughing. And then your privacy would be broken."

We found a keen awareness of the privacy risks presented by online life especially among the youngest of our interviewees. Moreover, most youths talked about using different strategies to manage these risks, ranging from the simple withholding of information and other content to a fine-tuned customization of privacy settings to more elaborate schemes in which multiple profiles are set up on Facebook or LiveJournal for different audiences. A 2013 study of the Berkman Center and the Pew Internet and American Life Project provides further data. The national survey and focus group study revealed that compared to the findings of earlier studies, youth are disclosing more information online; however, they are also using a variety of strategies to control the audiences for their content.[6]

Also important, however—and adding fuel to the fire for those who believe that "kids these days have no sense of privacy"—youth's privacy strategies are not always perfectly employed, but even when they are, they can be swiftly undercut by the actions of online friends. A major and obvious reason is that youth are interacting in contexts that enable, prize, and, to a large extent, *exist for* the sharing of information, photos, and thoughts with others. Accordingly, Facebook founder Mark Zuckerberg lauds "frictionless sharing" as a key virtue and goal of Facebook, which perpetually asks users, "What's on your mind?" and invites them to share with online "friends," "friends of friends," or "everyone."

Youth accept this invitation in part because online social networks are essential sites for participation in peer life—to many youths, having a Facebook, Tumblr, or Twitter account does not feel optional.[7] Those who don't participate may feel sidelined or "out of the loop" as plans are made, gossip is shared, memories are posted, and romances are kindled and broken—all online. The importance of peer communication, including reciprocal self-expression and validation, for social and identity development is well-understood.[8] Blogging, status updating, "liking," and commenting are online forms of carrying out these essential developmental tasks.[9]

Imprudent sharing on social network sites may also be influenced by the fact that capacities such as impulse control and future orientation are still developing in adolescence.[10] Similarly, the "disinhibition effect" associated with communicating through a screen may be at play.[11] Finally, beyond the obligatory, developmental, and technical aspects of participation, youth-populated online spaces—including blogging communities, social networks, and interest-based forums—can be engaging and empowering.[12] When 14-year-old Jonah talked about the appeal of the instant messaging program AIM, he described it as "a teenager world" in which he and his friends can privately share their frustrations about parents and teachers.

The desire to express oneself, fit in, and bond with peers in public or semipublic view online is often in tension with the potential risks of online sharing. Communications scholars Miriam Metzger and Rebekah Pure talk about the "privacy paradox"—the fact that social network sites present incentives and risks for disclosure—and argue that young people actively engage in "risk-benefit" assessments as they participate in these environments.[13] Similarly, Sonia Livingstone refers to the "risky opportunities" presented by social media.[14] A complex interplay of technological affordances, young people's psychosocial development, and peer dynamics contributes to both positive and ill-conceived online sharing by young people on social network sites.

Digital contexts therefore pose opportunities, challenges, and responsibilities in relation to privacy. How youth take up those responsibilities and with what mindsets are key questions. While it is heartening to know that young people care about privacy and are attuned to the related risks and rewards presented online, we need to ask to what extent their attention is alert to the *moral* and *ethical* issues versus keyed exclusively to the *personal* dilemmas and responsibilities.

As mentioned earlier, from our interviews with young people, we detected three distinct mindsets in relation to this landscape: privacy as social, privacy as "in your own hands," and privacy as forsaken. These mindsets appear with different levels of frequency and are sometimes in tension with one another in the approaches of individual young people. Below, I describe the key features of these mindsets. As you will see, the different mindsets involve different levels of alertness to the targets of thinking—self, known others, and distant others—and reveal the extent of moral and ethical sensitivity toward online privacy issues.

Privacy As Social

Among most of the young people we interviewed, we observed evidence of a desire for a social approach to online privacy. This desire most often appeared in the expectations the youths held about how their friends should handle *their* information and content. When Kayla, age 17, talked about online privacy, she said, "On Facebook, [privacy] means not having people show messages that I wouldn't want other people to know besides the person I send it to." Kayla's comment represents a self-focused angle on the "privacy as social" mindset. She counts on her friends not to violate *her* privacy. Similarly, Nora, age 19, is concerned about the consequences of her friends posting incriminating pictures and other content about her: "I also know that jobs nowadays look at Facebook and MySpace, and they can get me in trouble for things I'm not even posting."

A social approach to privacy hinges on trust. In their book *Born Digital*, John Palfrey and Urs Gasser argue that "the concept of trust is at the heart of the privacy issue on the internet."[15] Whereas Palfrey and Gasser focus on the commercial entities that imperil youth's privacy, the trust—sometimes thick, sometimes thin—between online and offline friends is a more salient aspect of young people's thinking. "Strong ties" online are accompanied by thick trust, which can nourish robust social approaches to privacy protection.[16]

Teen and young adult bloggers spoke about the intimate sharing that takes place on tight-knit, semiprivate blogging platforms. Eight tweens told us about explicit agreements they had made with friends, siblings, and even parents to protect and respect one another's privacy—agreeing not to look at one another's text messages, iChat conversations, or social network accounts. Maeve, age 11, described texting on her cell phone as "private" because "it's going to straight to [my friends] ... my best friends aren't going to forward stuff. And we have trust in each other that we're not going to forward things that we write. We're writing it to them, so they shouldn't show other people. It's just private." Maeve and her friends appear to have a social contract, built on trust, to protect one another's privacy online.

Other youths were mindful of the need to withhold certain types of content about friends from the Web. Caleb, age 10, said, "When you have a picture of someone and it's really bad, I would just erase it. And I would, if there was something bad, I wouldn't put the picture on my AIM or Gmail." Similarly Lam, age 21, considers the perspectives of his friends when he creates video mashups that feature them:

I guess for me the only taboo thing ... it never really seemed to me like such a big deal, I guess, but the one thing I just keep in mind is, these are my friends; I don't want to show them in the worst light. So I wouldn't do something that would overly embarrass them. I sort of consult them first to see if it's okay for me to use the clip of them doing this, or whatever [before] putting it on there. And I'd gladly take it down if they said they didn't like it.

Social privacy strategies such as these have the potential to address the limitations of technical settings and affordances that often compromise privacy online. Notably, the key principle underlying these approaches is respect.

Related to this, references to the social or moral dimensions of privacy appeared among just over half of teens and young adults and among nearly half of tweens. When asked about the norms among her close friends on LiveJournal, Nina, age 24, said, "The biggest one I can think of is not complaining about friends or maybe using [their] names." This way of thinking surfaced as well when youths talked about disrespectful online posting practices by their peers. Emma, age 20, told us, "It still troubles me when I see kids getting messed up and just showing pictures. Sometimes they'll show pictures of their friends without telling them. And then that's kind of messed up." Finally, 18-year-old Petra stated, "I feel you should respect somebody else, because you wouldn't want them doing it to you." Golden Rule thinking and imagining oneself in the shoes of the victim of a privacy invasion was a common way in which youths in our study showed moral sensitivity about privacy.

The "privacy as social" mindset surfaced largely in relation to strong ties or intimates. However, the large numbers of weak ties that young people collect on Facebook, MySpace, and Twitter—sometimes upwards of 1,000 people—mean that their expectations, and trust, of most online "friends" and "followers" are inevitably thin. Perhaps it should be no surprise, then, that young people's expectations of their friends were largely implicit and thus tenuous—often by their own admission. When asked whether he expected other people to respect his privacy online, Keith, age 23, responded, "I guess you can go in expecting that, but I don't necessarily know that that's going to happen with everybody. And I just feel like there's a lot of interesting ways people can see stuff even if they weren't actively searching and trying to invade your privacy."

An emerging social approach to the weak-tie privacy challenge—and the frequent changes on social network sites that make one's privacy vulnerable—is the growing use of status updates instructing online friends to adjust what they see in their news feeds and tickers about their friends' interactions with others, including "likes" and comments. These moves can be seen as community efforts to counter Zuckerberg's vision of "friction-less sharing." Moreover, such instructions make explicit which content an online friend considers to be private, semipublic, or public.

The "privacy as social" mindset has the potential to help counter the features of the Internet that often undercut intended privacy. Among the youths we studied, we found a desire for, if not an expectation of, respect for their privacy online. Among some of them, we also saw a willingness to reciprocate to others. Unfortunately, youth's privacy expectations are more often implicit than explicit. We saw efforts by some youths to create mutual expectations for the respect of privacy online, but these efforts were few and far between. There is a clear need for explicit social and moral agreements about privacy among both strong and weak online ties. However, other mindsets loom larger in the discourse about privacy among both youth and adults.

Privacy As "In Your Own Hands"

Internet safety rhetoric, often conveyed through the advice of parents and teachers and stories in the media, suggests quite strongly that what one does online "sticks" and may therefore come back to "bite" young people—potentially damaging their reputations and life chances. Youth express keen awareness of these risks, even while they enthusiastically participate and share in these central spaces of youth sociality. This privacy paradox most often leads to an approach focused on individualized strategies aimed at controlling what is shared and with whom.[17] Nearly all the youths we interviewed argued that, in large part, privacy is "in your own hands" online.

When Jess, age 22, was asked what she thinks about privacy on social networks, she remarked, "There isn't much privacy on Facebook, but it kind of is in your own hands." Among teens and young adults in particular, we observed this notably individualistic mantra. Citing a case in which Miss Nevada USA lost her title after risqué photos of her were posted on MySpace, 20-year-old Christina said, "She should have been on top of that and gotten rid of those pictures…. That is a big, high-profile example of [the need to] take care of yourself online. Take responsibility for it. It's in your hands. You have the ability to control what you do. And if you're stupid enough not to, well, that's your fault."

Despite the reality that social media are inherently interactive, this mindset views privacy as the responsibility of the individual featured in a given photo, video, or blog post—regardless of who posted it and the countless others who may have forwarded it. The blame-the-victim mentality of Christina and other youth is an extension of this mindset.

An important facet of the "in your own hands" mindset is that youth need to be proactive, making use of the technical settings available to them to limit the audiences for their online content. In speaking about these controls, Gavin, age 18, argued, "I think [that MySpace is] as private as you want to make it. Some kids are just horrible with it, and then they wonder why things happen.... I mean, you could put [personal] things, but then you've got to put the security or whatever on your site." Angela, age 21, even asserted that "Facebook cannot make privacy controls for you. You control your own privacy." Certainly a lot of young people have balked at the actions of Facebook and other sites, which have, at various points, compromised users' privacy in pursuit of their commercial interests. What Angela and other young adults in our study emphasized, however, is that their own actions are the baseline for privacy creation on these sites.

Consequently, we observed that most youths used one or more proactive privacy measures, such as adjusting technical privacy settings (most common), using private messaging, self-censoring (deleting content posted by oneself), censoring others (deleting content posted by others), creating pseudonyms, and lying about their age, city, or other biographical information.[18]

These individualized measures were in use among the tweens as well, although this younger age group was less autonomous in implementing them, since parents and older siblings were more involved in overseeing their online postings. Among tweens, we observed a remarkable naivete about the efficacy of these measures. When Zachary, age 12, was asked whether it's ever hard to create privacy online, he responded, "Nah, I know all the little tricks and stuff." A substantial minority of the youths, regardless of age, suggested that they didn't fully understand privacy settings and don't always use them effectively.[19]

The individual responsibility mantra also manifested when the youths criticized their peers for oversharing online. Although some young adults seek the spotlight that social media sites afford and admire others for seizing it, most of the young people we interviewed looked down on their peers for ill-conceived sharing. They talked about the inappropriateness of "ranting and raving in public," sharing emotions that other people "don't need to know," or foolishly posting pictures showing alcohol or illegal drug use.

The most widely discussed online privacy strategy was withholding or not disclosing personal information. The importance of withholding private, or potentially private, content about others was mentioned but was far less central in their approaches. We often observed a blind spot regarding the implications of one's online participation for others. Yet, a recent study showed that use of age deception by underage Facebook users (often with the advice or knowledge of their parents) can create privacy implications for friends. Youths who create a Facebook account with a fake age become "adults" online while they are still technically minors. Because Facebook has different policies for adult accounts and minor accounts, a premature shift to adult status makes the youths' information, including their "friends" lists, searchable even though they are still minors.[20]

What is not surprising about the "in your own hands" approach to online privacy is its link to the broader ethos of individualism prevalent in American culture. For issues ranging from academic achievement to employment and career success to being overweight, the belief that the "buck stops" at the individual is insidious—despite powerful counterarguments and evidence of the social influences on individual outcomes.[21] What is especially peculiar about the individual responsibility mindset vis-à-vis online privacy is that it flies so clearly in the face of the deeply social nature of online spaces—and the limited amount of control one can actually have over one's digital footprint.

Many teens and young adults acknowledged that the actions of others, including friends, peers, and strangers, either did or could undercut their privacy. Yet they still clung to privacy being "in my own hands" as the operative approach. The overwhelming amount of attention to personal responsibility in these interactive contexts amounts to a blind spot—a failure to see how one's actions and fate are interwined with those of others and to assume the associated social and moral responsibilities.

Privacy As Forsaken

Another theme that surfaced in our interviews with young people was the idea that on a fundamental level, privacy is impossible to attain online.

This view is in obvious tension with the "in your own hands" mindset and with the strong desire to have some semblance of privacy either through technical controls or through social agreements with others. Importantly, it also suggests that privacy can't be achieved through an ethos of social and moral responsibility.

The core belief guiding this mindset is that once information or content is posted online, it's "up for grabs." That is, if one creates a Facebook, Twitter, or Tumblr account—with or without privacy settings—one is essentially forsaking a right to privacy. Put in legal terms, a "reasonable expectation of privacy" cannot necessarily be maintained as soon as one elects to participate in online communities.[22]

A little more than half of the tweens (52 percent) and teens and young adults (55 percent) that we interviewed asserted that privacy is diminished online. Jared, age 24, said, "Online you almost give up your privacy. When you send an email, that email is actually the property of Yahoo or Gmail or whoever, or Harvard or the museum, whoever's site you're using. I mean, typically they're not going to look at those things, but, you know, they have that right."

Twelve-year-old Makayla similarly argued that "basically anything in the cyberspace is, when you put it on something electronic, it's gone. Your privacy is pretty much gone." Max, age 14, even went so far as to say that the public nature of online life has led him to value his own privacy less:

I don't really think [privacy] means much anymore at this point. I mean, privacy to me is—most of my life is very public, and I know that. If someone had the administrative authority, they could go in my account and find out a lot about me, if they wanted to. In some ways, that's sort of, it's a little bit scary. But in some ways I sort of like the fact that how you think and how you feel is very public and very presented to people and it's right up front.

Unlike Max, most youth are not resigned to leading public lives, and they take as many precautions as possible—at least in relation to their own online content—despite recognizing that these strategies give them limited control.

Although an awareness of privacy risks can lead to more prudent behavior online, the "privacy as forsaken" mindset can also contribute to privacy lapses by youth and adults alike. In our interviews, we observed a small number of cases in which youths had intentionally, and egregiously, invaded the privacy of others online. One teen, Kayla, shared that her friends had created a fake Facebook profile in order to "friend" their hockey coach and access her Facebook page, thus invading her privacy. Describing the situation as "just really funny," Kayla evinced the attitude that the privacy of their coach's online information was forsaken, despite the "friends only" privacy setting that the coach had chosen in order to protect it.

A college student, Carlos, age 21, revealed that he had accessed his girlfriend's Facebook account behind her back and read her private messages. Although he acknowledged, after the fact, that he was the culprit of a privacy invasion, in the moment, when faced with the Facebook log-in screen that contained her saved password, he simply clicked Log In and began to search and read. Ironically, Carlos's somewhat cavalier attitude about his girlfriend's privacy stands in sharp contrast to his strict ethical stance about online property, specifically music piracy.

Here we observe a different kind of disconnect in ethical ways of thinking for different themes or types of decisions confronted online. Overall, the privacy invasions these youths discussed alluded to an implicit sense that if it is technically possible to access information and other content online, then it is acceptable to do so.

More frequent than the egregious cases were instances in which many youths failed to consider their friends' potential reactions to being tagged in photos or featured in videos posted online. Nineteen-year-old Serena described how she posted a video featuring her roommate on Facebook: "With my roommate, sometimes she'll do really obnoxious things. She was dancing around or something in the room once. It wasn't anything bad; it was just dancing. And I was recording and she didn't notice, and I posted it. And later she went and saw it and she just detagged it." The roommate's untagging indicated her disapproval of the posting, something that Serena had failed to consider in advance.

Consistent with this is the thinking that certain online disclosures, such as the posting of party pictures on Facebook, are simply expected among peers and therefore unstoppable. As Hannah, a college student, put it, "If you're going to a party, people have cameras, you're going to be on Facebook, you're going to be on MySpace." Kristen, age 24, agreed that automatic photo posting is routine among her peers and added, "Also, I think, even relatively embarrassing photos that you wouldn't want up otherwise are really pretty commonly posted, regardless of your feelings."

Underlying these acts is the sense that since their peers have elected to be on MySpace, Facebook, or blogs, they must *want* to be photographed, tagged, and viewed—or at least accept this loss of control as part of the social network site bargain. The fact that youth's expectations of how others will handle their privacy are often implicit, as noted above, can contribute to such lapses.

We can also detect the "privacy as forsaken" mindset in high-profile cases in which publicity via social media is used as a weapon or a vehicle for relational aggression. In a 2012 case, Ariane Friedrich, a German Olympic-level athlete, posted the name and address of an online stalker on her Facebook page as a revenge tactic. Her fans were split over whether this tit-for-tat approach was appropriate, and the controversy was heightened by strict German online privacy laws.[23]

In another controversial case, described in the previous chapter, Rutgers University student Dharun Ravi used a webcam on two occasions to view his roommate, Tyler Clementi, having sexual relations with a male partner. Ravi invited his friends to watch and shared details with his Twitter followers.[24]

Both the Friedrich and Ravi cases involve privacy invasions that, in different ways, pose harm to their targets. Intentionally or not, the acts also convey to broader audiences (Facebook friends and Twitter followers, in these cases) that such invasions are acceptable, or "fair game." After he was convicted of privacy invasion and related charges, Ravi apologized for his "thoughtless, insensitive … choices … which at no time were motivated by hate, bigotry, prejudice, or desire to hurt, humiliate, or embarrass anyone, [but] were nonetheless the wrong choices and decisions."[25] Ravi's apology and admission of "thoughtlessness" suggest a blind spot at the time of his actions.

There may be many instances in which digital affordances—what we *can* do with the technologies—are seized without due consideration of whether we *should* do certain things. However, to be clear, digital media do not *cause* youth to believe that privacy is forsaken and to commit such acts. Psychological, social, and cultural forces are far more powerful factors in such failures of empathy and ethics.[26]

Turning to less tragic examples, we also see the growing norm of using Google and other search engines to look up information about people—information which, whether credible or fictitious, may be used as a basis for making hiring, dating, and business decisions.[27] One young adult shared that her employer asks her to conduct online searches for personal information about clients before meeting them. Although she acknowledged this practice to be "creepy," she fulfills her boss's request.

Another young adult, Alexis, told us, "Privacy is nonexistent online.... Okay, where in the past, where in history has anybody been able to Google Earth their ex's house, okay? Or punch in for a people search and find somebody's phone number? Or find out when or where they were married, or all these things, for free, very easily?" The suggestion here is that the capacity to dig up information about another person weakens, if not undercuts entirely, any expectations of privacy.

Crucially, lapses facilitated by the "privacy as forsaken" mindset can weaken the individualized privacy strategies that most young people embrace. More important, given my focus here, is that the implications for the "privacy as social" mindset and the moral approach, based on respect, are even more troubling. Here we have another disconnect: the belief that an expectation of privacy is untenable and unreasonable on the Web is at odds with the clear desire young people have for their own privacy on social media sites and in other spaces. Furthermore, the "privacy as forsaken" mindset can contribute to a general ethos of *dis*respect of others' privacy in new media environments.

Accounting for Privacy Blind Spots and Disconnects

In this chapter, I have considered how youth think about online privacy, paying particular attention to the degree to which they show moral and ethical sensitivity when they discuss this topic. Although some youths acknowledge these aspects of privacy, individualistic modes of thinking about privacy more often dominate their concerns. A variety of factors are at play here. Below, I discuss how such thinking gaps, including both blind spots and disconnects, may be fed by the qualities of digital technologies and environments, developmental factors, peer norms, and messages from adults and from the broader culture.

Young people in our studies certainly expressed an awareness of the unique qualities of digital content—especially its persistence, replicability, and the related risks of its discovery by unintended audiences. Awareness of these qualities can certainly increase youth's sensitivity to the *personal* risks of social media use, which in turn feeds a desire to exert as much control as possible over their privacy, as epitomized by the pervasive mindset that privacy is "in your own hands."

However, many youths were less attentive, sometimes even blind, to these qualities when they shared information and content about others. The perpetual invitation to share, built into social media and other online platforms, is relevant here. As I discuss in the concluding chapter, it's worth considering how social media companies might assist in correcting these blind spots. Yet the mindful disconnects require other interventions. Some youth who embraced the resigned "privacy as forsaken" mindset evinced such disconnects, leveraging the Internet's openness to invade others' privacy.

The qualities and features of social media platforms and other online spaces can influence our dispositions to share more than we should about ourselves and others. However, the qualities alone don't drive privacy blind spots and disconnects. Rather, there is a complex interplay of these qualities, psychological factors, and the social norms we confront in these spaces. In adolescence, the ability to project into the future is still developing, which can lead to ill-conceived sharing.[28]

Furthermore, when youth are in the prime stages of identity development in which self-presentation, self-disclosure, and the pursuit of peer feedback are central, they are drawn to highly social spaces.[29] Studies show that young people increasingly feel compelled to participate.[30] In a recent article aptly entitled, "Facebook Made Me Do It," Jenna Wortham describes how the pull of immediate social approval often leads people to share with abandon.[31] The kinds of things their friends share contribute by setting the norm for what is appropriate.

When the expectation, or social fact, is that all social events will be documented on Instagram, it's not surprising that many youth snap and upload without warranted consideration for how others might feel. As the inclination to share becomes habitual, reflection may be deferred or skipped altogether. Peers may exert the strongest influence on young people's decisions and mindsets about online privacy. However, youth are also recipients (even if not always attentive ones) of messages from adults and from the broader culture.

The Word from Adults: What Youth Hear about Online Privacy

When we asked the youths about their conversations with adults (parents, teachers, and other influential adult figures) about online privacy issues, two distinct stories emerged.

The teens and young adults reported little direct dialogue with adults on these issues, although some noted that their schools had conducted assemblies about Internet safety in which privacy issues were raised. Media influences were also cited—including high-profile stories of online risks often featured on the television program *To Catch a Predator*.

From tweens, we heard that much more dialogue was taking place at school and especially at home. Tweens told us that their parents were overseers of their online lives; the parents often insisted on being "friends" with their children on social networks, approving content before it was posted online, and monitoring their profiles on an ongoing basis.[32]

The messages that youth get from these Internet conversations—including the school assemblies mentioned by teens and young adults—are telling. We heard of strong support from adults for individualized approaches to privacy protection (privacy as "in your own hands"), often bolstered by fear-based tactics emphasizing the risks to privacy in a connected world (privacy as forsaken).

More specifically, the dominant messages heard by youth were focused on the adverse consequences of oversharing online, the foremost being "stranger danger" and being refused a job or admission to a school because of inappropriate online content. Leah, a high school student, shared, "Mostly the school is really big on warning us about, you know, 'Careful what you're doing at parties, because people have cameras and colleges could see. And then you couldn't get into college. Or the authorities [might see]. Or you don't get a job.'"

Tweens reported hearing frequent "stranger danger" messages from parents and getting related help in handling personal information in their online profiles. Although most tweens were advised to post little or no information, three tweens told us that their parents encouraged deception as a privacy measure. Kevin, age 11, told us, "My mommy knows that I have a Facebook or MySpace, ... [and] she always tells me to change my age, just in case of people online." We found it notable that in all our interviews, only one youth mentioned an adult speaking with her about the social, moral, or ethical dimensions of online privacy.

When we spoke with adults about managing their own privacy, their narratives showed significant concerns with the risks posed to privacy by new media environments and technologies. The "privacy as forsaken" mindset is very prevalent among parents and teachers, and so is attention to the precautions that they (and their students or children) should take, in line with the "in your own hands" mindset. In other words, what we heard from adults was not dramatically different from what we heard from youth. Adults' attitudes about online privacy didn't contain much more sensitivity to moral and ethical concerns than the youths' attitudes did. Although more adults spoke with eloquence about the need for greater consideration and respect for others' privacy, on balance, adults, like the youths, were mainly preoccupied with personal consequences. Moreover, adults' messages to youth were sharply focused on safety and self-protective measures. Our data therefore point to a mentorship gap in relation to the moral and ethical dimensions of privacy in a digital age.

As I noted earlier in the chapter, the focus on the individual as the locus of responsibility for privacy is characteristically American. The self-focused ways of thinking, mindsets, and messages about online privacy that surfaced in interviews with youth and adults are not surprising; they are tightly aligned with long-held and deeply cherished beliefs about how we conduct our lives.

Conclusion

In the popular media, the "end of privacy" discourse prevails. As a result, there is much talk today about managing one's "digital footprint" or "digital dossier." Unfortunately, the discourse generated by all this discussion focuses largely on the personal risks and encourages individualized—and ultimately, insufficient—approaches to a complex, deeply social, even moral problem. Overall, how we think about online privacy and the risk of overexposure has to extend beyond concern for our own reputations. Our thinking must take into account the deeply social nature of the Web and our moral and ethical responsibilities in our roles as online information sharers, searchers, and consumers.

How young people and adults alike approach online privacy dilemmas is a matter of character. Moreover, our approaches, in aggregate, are dictating the kind of world we live in. On the one hand, we have the very real possibility of creating a world of no second chances. In such a future, youth may be completely risk-averse, seeking to avoid making mistakes at all costs and striving to bury the evidence when they do.[33] On the other hand, some thinkers suggest that ultimately we will need to create a more forgiving world—at the very least, in relation to gaffes committed by children before they are old enough to be aware of the potential consequences.

Although many employers consider it just plain prudent to conduct Internet searches on job candidates, there are indications that others take an "eyes wide shut" approach to hiring that conceives of online content as private, even though technically public. As Jeffrey Rosen argues, "As all of us stumble over the challenges of living in a world without forgetting, we need to learn new forms of empathy, new ways of defining ourselves without reference to what others say about us and new ways of forgiving one another for the digital trails that will follow us forever."[34]

In this chapter, I have explored the ways of thinking that youth exhibit about online privacy. The dominance of individualized mindsets and consequence-oriented ways of thinking about privacy contributes to both moral and ethical blind spots about privacy. Moreover, the prevalent belief that privacy is forsaken online can contribute to failures to consider the moral and ethical consequences of using digital tools to access others' private lives.

Amid these disheartening trends, however, we also observe a clear desire on the part of youth to have their own privacy respected by others and that some youths embrace the mindset that online privacy is a social, even moral, matter. The conscientious habits of connectivity exemplified by these youths expand our sense of how privacy may be managed and preserved in an increasingly public world. These findings suggest the need for a new discourse about online privacy one that balances personal risk with sensitivity to the social, moral, and ethical dimensions of privacy in a digital age.

Encouraging the mindset that privacy is a social enterprise may require a dramatic shift in perspective. In the United States in particular, our tendency may be to think about the private as the information that relates to and belong to us, as individuals, that we aim to keep from others. However, if one considers the fact that we have always shared sensitive information with a select few under the assumption that they would protect it, we can see how our notions of privacy have carried social dimensions all along. Acknowledging the features of online environments that limit the amount of control an individual has over his or her privacy is an opportunity to rethink privacy as a social enterprise.

Avner Levin and Patricia Sanchez Abril argue for a "privacy as dignity" model, a foundational aspect of privacy law in Europe, which is based on respect for the dignity of others.[35] Although some youth are crafting impressive strategies that suggest that privacy is a matter of dignity, it is crucial that the burden of rethinking privacy in these ways not lie on youth alone. This rethinking must also be done by adults—parents, educators, Internet safety curriculum purveyors, and the designers and executives behind social media sites—who are poised to influence how youth approach these matters. An important first step in achieving this is to give equal weight to moral responsibility and citizenship as we give to personal responsibility and safety in Internet conversations with youth.

3 Property

The Wikipedian's Dilemma

Imagine you have a long-standing interest in economic development in Latin America and have been both reading and contributing to Wikipedia articles about Latin America for several months. Your history teacher recently assigned a research paper about poverty in Brazil, and you start your research by looking at the relevant Wikipedia article. Much of the article is content that you wrote a couple of months ago, and with the added work of other Wikipedia contributors, it has become very detailed and thoroughly cited. With a few adjustments here and there, the Wikipedia article would perfectly fulfill your teacher's assignment. How, if at all, would you use it for your research paper?

If you are like more than half of Internet-connected Americans, Wikipedia is your go-to source, or at least your first stop, for quick information on the Web.[1] You may not fully trust it, but perhaps you look to it nonetheless for a high-level overview of a momentary topic of interest (What's photosynthesis, again?) or for basic facts about events or individuals (When was John Lennon shot?). The purposes for which we turn to Wikipedia, or the stakes of the information we are pursuing, often determine how we use the information, including whether we dig deeper, triangulate sources, and critically reflect on what we find there.

Similarly, for students, Wikipedia has become *the* source of choice for homework assignments and research papers, at least for getting started on them. A 2009 study of college students at six American universities found that 52 percent "frequently" or "always" turned to Wikipedia as a support for course-related research. Qualities of the site, including its convenience and coverage, were cited as important factors in its popularity as a research tool.[2]

In our study, 72 percent of the teens and young adults and 67 percent of the tweens reported having used Wikipedia for a school assignment or research paper. The use of Wikipedia is also prevalent among older adults, especially the highly educated.[3] Among the well-educated group of parents and teachers we interviewed, nearly half reported frequent use of the online encyclopedia.

An impressive number of young people have become involved as editors of Wikipedia, or Wikipedians, as they call themselves. According to a 2010 multinational survey, youth between the ages of 10 and 21 make up nearly half of the contributors. In our study, we found comparatively lower but still impressive numbers: nearly 33 percent of the teens and young adults and 12 percent of the tweens reported that they had either edited or started a Wikipedia entry. These youth are involved to various degrees; most have made only small additions or corrections to a single page, but a few have contributed substantial content to numerous pages over time.

The popularity of Wikipedia as an information source, its digital and open form, and its collaborative nature combine to make it an opportune topic for probing youth's notions of intellectual property, coauthorship, proper use of information sources, and related ethical questions. In the research paper scenario above, we placed these issues alongside one another, assuming that Wikipedia would be the go-to information source for a research paper but adding the twist that the student had also been a contributor to the Wikipedia content in question. We sought to understand to what extent youth considered the content they had contributed to be "theirs," at least in part, and their related sense of obligation to other contributors. We also aimed to elicit their views about whether and how it was acceptable to repurpose such content for a different context.

"What's Mine Is Mine": Youth Respond

We presented this scenario to a sample of 24 teens and young adults in our study.[4] Their responses suggest that many youth still adhere to the notion of a single author and owner, even of text found in explicitly collaborative contexts such as Wikipedia. Most youth considered the text they had added to Wikipedia to be "theirs." Even so, the courses of action they proposed in the scenario varied.

Only two youths, or 8 percent of the group, would copy and paste the Wikipedia entry and submit it as is or with minor modification. More than 33 percent said that they would "disentangle" the text they had written from other Wikipedians' contributions so that they would use only their own writing for the paper.

Finally, nearly 60 percent of the youths said that they would use the Wikipedia entry only as a starting point from which to learn and identify additional resources for writing the assigned paper. The fact that the overwhelming majority would not simply turn in a copy of the Wikipedia page as their paper suggests the presence of a strong ethical code in relation to collaborative authorship and academic integrity. However, if we look more closely at the reasoning underpinning the responses, we find that many youths were *in*sensitive to the scenario's ethical dimensions.

Indeed, just over half of the teens and young adults viewed the scenario principally through a self-focused, consequence-oriented lens. The potential negative consequences of misusing the Wikipedia text, the foremost one being getting a poor grade on the paper, loomed large for these youths. Justine, age 19, revealed a sharp focus on the consequences to herself when she said, "It's kind of a catch-22. It's like, I'm not going to use all this information that I worked hard on. Or I'm going to get in trouble or just get a 'not valid' for using Wikipedia."

A concern for the amount of time previously invested in the Wikipedia entry underpinned the responses of several youth who would either submit the entire entry or the specific text they had written. The thinking expressed by Peter, age 20, was "Why do the work twice?" Peter appears to feel a sense of ownership over, and entitlement to, the work he contributed to Wikipedia and prioritizes his time over other possible considerations. This stance may be understandable in light of mounting academic pressures on young people today. Nevertheless, the view is at odds with the ethos of Wikipedia: to contribute knowledge for the common good, without expectation of credit or reward.

Although the consequence-focused approach was a bit more prevalent, moral or ethical concerns were on the minds of just under half of the youths responding to the Wikipedia scenario. Explaining why she would not use the Wikipedia entry for her paper, 19-year-old Leah said, "Well, it would be plagiarism, since other people have contributed." Like Leah, youths who prioritized the moral dimensions of this scenario pointed to, and took the perspectives of, other stakeholders: either other contributors whose work might be inappropriately used or other students in the class who set out to do the assignment from scratch, as intended by the teacher.

Trey, age 15, was sensitive to the effects on his classmates: "For all the people in the class who did work on the project ... and spent months on it, that's like ripping them off." Explicit moral principles and beliefs about academic integrity were also evident among this group. Jared, age 24, explained, "I see it as morally wrong to do that stuff." Yolanda, age 23, said that whereas some of her friends have actually submitted excerpts from Wikipedia for school assignments, she and other friends "have a conscience." One youth extended conscientious thinking even further, considering the scenario's broader ethical dimensions. He discussed academia as a system based on trusting people to treat and cite others' work with care. Without that sense of trust and respect, he said, the system loses integrity.

Young people's responses to the Wikipedia scenario also give us insight into their views about the ethics of repurposing. Just over half of the youth with whom we shared this scenario felt that resubmitting an old paper for a new class did not amount to wrongdoing. The ethics of reusing one's own work can be a gray area even for professional writers. In July 2012, Jonah Lehrer resigned from the *New Yorker* magazine after admitting to fabricating quotes and using his previous writings for allegedly new articles. Granted, the question of when an ethical line is crossed by using one's own previous written work can be vague. However, practices such as acknowledging the previous work through citation—making the reader aware that the ideas have been presented elsewhere in a similar form—are often standard for written work.

Overall, the Wikipedia scenario revealed that most of the youths felt some attachment to text they had written, even in a coauthorship context. However, with a few exceptions, they understood that a Wikipedia entry to which they had contributed was not simply theirs for the taking. Perhaps even more interesting was the underlying thinking here. The youths with whom we spoke were in one of two camps: slightly more than half viewed the scenario in purely consequence-oriented terms ("I might get into trouble if I use the entry"), and just under half perceived the question as a moral or ethical dilemma ("It's not right to use the entry").

The implications of these very different ways of thinking are worth considering. How youth think about these issues is arguably significant if we aim to inspire them to participate both meaningfully and respectfully in emerging collaborative contexts. Respect and conscience may be a more meaningful and reliable basis than consequence thinking for handling cocreated content with care.

Although this chapter is entitled "Property," I address two related but distinct topics: (1) crediting sources when one creates (which is not a legal property issue, strictly speaking), and (2) considering and respecting the stakes (copyright as well as other nonlegal interests) of content creators, owners, users, and other constituencies. In what follows, I explore the considerations that guide youth's thinking about accessing and using a range of content—text, images, video, or music—and the broader mindsets that support their thinking.

First I describe a range of related dilemmas posed in the digital age. I then discuss two sometimes conflicting mindsets that appear in the youths' approaches to such dilemmas and show how these mindsets surface in their narratives about the citation of text, the use of playful online content, and the downloading of music and film. Finally, I consider how technological affordances as well as developmental, social, and cultural factors (including messages and signals from adults) contribute to the ways of thinking about property observed among the youths.

Property in a Digital Age: The Dilemmas

The Wikipedian example and other intellectual property scenarios point to a core set of dilemmas with heightened salience in the digital age: access and attribution, remix, and cocreation. These dilemmas are examined below.

Access and Attribution Dilemmas

The Internet and the nearly ubiquitous devices we use to browse it afford a new level of access to information and other content. As we stroll through a park with our smartphones or tablets, we can access clips from *Seinfeld* courtesy of YouTube, historical facts about the Cuban Missile Crisis via Wikipedia, and photos of Lindsay Lohan's latest escapades on People.com.

This access is anytime and, before too long, will be anywhere as Internet coverage continues to extend across the globe, even into its deep rural pockets. The Web is a seductive treasure trove of news, information, and entertainment content. A lot of this content is made available for free, becoming part of a growing digital commons. However, some online content is not "up for grabs"—or at least not intentionally so. Therefore, there are both legal and ethical dimensions to how we access content on the Web.

It is important to note that the legal and the ethical are not synonymous. The legality of an act is not a reliable indicator of its ethical status. The ethical status of copyright law is a topic of debate—especially considering the profits often reaped by the creative industries, the potential for hampering innovation by restricting content, and broader concerns about public access to cultural goods. The ease with which copyright laws can be breached through digital means, both intentionally and unintentionally, is increasing the intensity of such debates.

My particular interest is in the moral and ethical thinking behind, and the implications of, how we access, regard, and treat other people's content. To what extent does an act of appropriation indicate an appreciation of the work that a creator undertook and a consideration of the possible effects on his or her livelihood? Also relevant is the impact of how we access and share content on the integrity of a larger system or domain of creative work. Some illegal acts of appropriation are motivated by and constitute ethical challenges to unfair systems that are at odds with the public good.

The late Internet freedom activist Aaron Swartz is an exemplar here. Motivated by the belief that information should be free, in 2010 and early 2011, Swartz used MIT's network to download millions of scholarly articles from a restricted academic database. Some acts are thus aimed at disrupting the workings of a larger system—its operational integrity—in order to promote greater ethical integrity. Swartz argued that copyright violations motivated by such concerns are acts of civil disobedience.[5]

Similarly, sociologist Matthew David described file sharing as "'perestroika' and 'glasnost' from below: an economical restructuring and informational open-up that challenges capitalist relations of intellectual property."[6]

Again, my particular focus is on the thinking behind our choices: our sensitivity to the local and distant effects of particular acts. From the well-understood prohibition of plagiarism, and perhaps by a recognition of the meaning behind attribution, we may be attuned to the need to cite sources in written work submitted for a grade or for publication. Yet do we feel compelled to cite sources when we draw on content for social or expressive purposes—when we blog or create amusing tweets and Facebook status updates?

The same questions can be asked about visual and audio content. Do we provide source information for photographs culled from a Google image search for use in school assignments, presentations, or blog posts? What about pictures we use to adorn our social network site profiles? If we can readily access our favorite band's latest song or album through a free but illegal site, should we do so, and what kind of thinking guides our decision? A related concern is the extent to which we seek out, understand, and give weight to the intentions and concerns of musicians and photographers when we access their content. Finally, how do our purposes for obtaining content—profit versus play, a graded research paper versus an art club project—affect our thinking about ethical use of others' work?

These issues are certainly made more complex by the confusing mix of open-source, pay-for-access, and illegal sites on the Internet. The Web offers a compelling platter of content, often without lucid information about creators' and owners' rights and *intentions* regarding access and use.[7] Moreover, because online content often becomes disconnected from the site to which it was originally uploaded, the identities of its creators and owners may be lost or require significant effort to track down.

Remix Dilemmas

Further dilemmas arise as we consider the ways in which digital technologies allow us to mash up and remix content. The digital forms of music, video, and the like—the "bits" described by Nicholas Negroponte in *Being Digital*—allow content to be copied, remixed, and distributed with relative ease and often without loss of quality.[8] The creative affordances of digital media for youth are discussed by many authors.[9]

There is a growing recognition that producing and posting video mash-ups and other content on Tumblr or YouTube constitute new modes of participation in the public sphere. Creative (and often comedic) depictions of politicians and other power holders in society may amount to acts of "participatory politics"—especially when they become full-blown Internet memes poised to influence public discourse and opinion.[10] Within an hour of Mitt Romney's "binders full of women" remark in the second presidential debate of 2012, cleverly Photoshopped images of women in binders were circulating on all the major social media sites.

Yet as amusing, compelling, and powerful as some of these creative expressions may be, they also often involve the unattributed use of others' photos, music, and videos. The content may also feature unconsenting minors or raise other privacy concerns, especially if it "goes viral."

Certainly all works—no matter how original they may seem—are influenced by previous work. And retellings of well-known works from new perspectives are an established creative practice in literature, film, and theater. For example, *The Wizard of Oz* has inspired numerous remixes, including a best-selling novel, *Wicked*, that retells the story from a new perspective; the novel has also been adapted for a successful Broadway musical. With some adaptations, however, legal and ethical questions have arisen about the line between inspiration and plagiarism and the rights of a creator vis-à-vis the afterlife of his or her original work. In 2001, a court battle ensued over whether Alice Randall's *The Wind Done Gone*, a retelling of Margaret Mitchell's *Gone with the Wind* from the point of view of a freed slave, encroached on the copyright held by Mitchell's estate. Ultimately, Randall's retelling was deemed to be a legitimate parody and therefore a case of "fair use."[11]

These issues clearly predate the Internet. Yet in facilitating access to others' works and offering copy, paste, and download features, the Internet may present dilemmas more often and actually increase the likelihood of misappropriations if such situations are not perceived and engaged with as dilemmas. Digital technologies offer creative opportunities yet also often raise questions about ethical and fair use. As Henry Jenkins has persuasively argued, the Internet "lowers barriers" to creation and engenders empowering "participatory cultures" in which remixes and other transformative works, such as fan fiction, thrive.[12]

J. K. Rowling's Harry Potter series has spawned numerous fan fiction sites and at times raised the hackles of Warner Brothers, the copyright holders of the Harry Potter franchise.[13] Even though much of fan fiction has been appropriately deemed fair use, ethical questions should be considered as fans draw on and put their own spin on beloved works. How much, and what parts, of a story, song, or film are acceptable to draw on as is, and how much should be changed or added? That is, when is a remix simply derivative versus offering something new?

The legal concepts of *fair use* and *transformative use* correspond, to a certain extent, with my interest in the moral and ethical aspects of remixing. The principle of transformative use can be a helpful guide in dealing with these questions, but the answers aren't always clear-cut—and, more important, the questions might not even be asked in the first place.[14]

We should also consider the dilemmas from a different angle, examining when intellectual property rights that prevent the use of source material unfairly stifle creativity and innovation and thereby detract from the public good.[15] The extent to which these kinds of considerations are in our minds, and those of youth as they consume content and engage in creative activities, is the key point.

Cocreation Dilemmas

Finally, the interactive and participatory nature of the Web also affords new opportunities for collaboration in knowledge and creative coproduction. Sites like Wikipedia and open-source software programs may negate, or at least strain, conventional notions of ownership and authorship. Questions about how we treat the fruits of work we've coproduced require deliberation. Given our role in the creative process, we may consider the products to be ours to use as we like. Yet our cocreators may desire both permission for new use and warranted credit.

Digital contexts—with their copy, paste, download, remix, and collaborative features—vex conventional notions of authorship and ownership. Whether or not we acknowledge it, we routinely face dilemmas about how we access and use online content—with or without attribution, payment, or consideration of the original creators, owners, or cocreators. Competing views about property abound along with widespread ambiguity (if not outright conflict) about what is ethical and fair use. Youth's views on these issues, and the extent to which they are approaching this evolving landscape with sensitivity to the dilemmas, may indicate a need for more nuanced conversations about attribution and property in the digital age.

Of Two Minds

Overall, the youths with whom we spoke appear to have multiple mindsets about the property dilemmas raised in new media environments. That is, their ethical mindsets and approaches shift as they confront different appropriation scenarios involving different types of content and purposes of use. There is some evidence that their mindsets also shift as they occupy different roles in such scenarios. To a certain extent, this is appropriate, even desirable. Contextual features *should* matter in how we approach any given appropriation scenario.

However, too often, the most salient factor to youth is what they as individuals may gain or lose in the deal. For example, some youth will hold a more stringent ethical stance about content they created only to evince a more lax ethical stance regarding the use of other people's material. In other words, youth's mindsets are rarely disinterested. Two mindsets are most often featured and interchanged: a "what's theirs is theirs and what's mine is mine" mindset that coheres with intellectual property rights along with a more permissive free-for-all mindset.

Young people's comments about a range of intellectual property scenarios reveal an appreciation of the notion that a creator owns and therefore has certain rights over his or her original content. We observed variants of this mindset that reflected different levels of moral or ethical sensitivity. Some youth articulate robust ethically sensitive arguments for attribution and for respecting the rights of creators to have a say in how their works are accessed and used. More often, however, we observed greater sensitivity to the legal or penal aspects of intellectual property rights: "what's theirs is theirs," but more important was "if I take it, I might be punished."

The free-for-all mindset, in contrast, deemphasizes concepts such as authorship and ownership or at least challenges their integrity and relevance, especially in digital contexts. Like the "what's theirs is theirs" stance, this mindset takes various forms. A small number of youth put forth sophisticated, ethical arguments about "free culture" as a key ingredient of a good society. However, most young people's thinking is focused narrowly on their own needs and circumstances as users seeking specific content. The special affordances of digital content are sometimes a feature of this thinking, too: if it *can* be easily accessed, copied, downloaded, and adapted, it must be acceptable to do so.

Below, I discuss how these dueling and often disconnected mindsets surface when youth consider their use of written information sources, creative content shared on interest-based Web sites, and copyright-protected music and videos.

Copy, Paste, Cite? Using Online Text

When youth talk about the use of others' written work for school and work assignments, the "what's theirs is theirs" mindset dominates. Most youth have clearly internalized the prohibition on outright copying and voice a "must cite sources" mantra. However, as with the Wikipedian's dilemma, when we probe more deeply into the motivations for citation and not plagiarizing, we find more evidence of a concern for getting into trouble than for paying respect to an author's ideas.

For example, when we spoke with teens and young adults about their use of online sources for school or work, 70 percent of them prioritized consequence-oriented concerns. Ian, age 23, said, "Plagiarism—if you get caught doing it, especially at my college, it's a big offense. I could get kicked out or get an F in my class or something.... I admit I've probably not cited some things that I've put in my paper. But most of the time when I do that, I change it, so it's not officially plagiarism." Ian's thinking is keyed exclusively to the "official" prohibitions, which he follows (at least, "most of the time") in order to avoid negative sanctions.

It was notable, however, that young bloggers were more likely to be attuned to the moral and ethical dimensions of these issues than nonbloggers. Some of them explicitly compared noncitation to stealing. Neal, a 17-year-old music and technology blogger, explained, "If I take an image from something, or if I take an opinion from another blog, I'll do my best to give them credit. I'm not going to pretend that it was my own thought." Neal's conception of attribution as a moral obligation is noteworthy.

Similarly, a recent large-scale survey study showed that attribution is a top ethical value held by both personal and topical bloggers.[16] It is significant that youths involved in online writing show considerable moral or ethical sensitivity to authorship and ownership issues. Yet it is also notable that this sensitivity was rarer among the larger group of youths we interviewed, most of whom were principally engaged in friendship-driven activities such as online socializing, not content creation.[17]

Indeed, for most youth, concerns about failing a paper or a class typically outweigh, and often overwhelm, ethical considerations. The mindset of "what's theirs is theirs" is a gesture to others that carries a greater preoccupation with avoiding penalties for oneself. At the end of this chapter, I will discuss how adult messages perpetuate (and in some cases give rise to) this apparent blind spot regarding the moral and ethical dimensions of appropriation.

In terms of the free-for-all mindset, none of the youths with whom we spoke explicitly argued that it was acceptable to copy others' written work for school or work assignments. However, a few young adults described practices that correspond with that mindset—including paraphrasing others' writing without attribution and submitting it as their own. Related to this, recent studies suggest that the rate of plagiarism through copying and pasting material is on the rise among youth and may be related to casual attitudes toward appropriation in general.[18]

A qualitative study of middle school students found copy-and-paste plagiarism from the Internet to be routine, facilitated by the ease of copying and peer support for the practice as well as by "underdeveloped" notions of plagiarism.[19] In a 2012 survey by the Josephson Institute of Ethics, 32 percent of high school students reported copying one or more documents from the Internet for school assignments.[20] A recent book entitled *Cheating in College* reports that 39 percent of college students "consider cut-and-paste plagiarism from the internet either not cheating at all or just trivial cheating."[21] The tendency to trivialize this practice is even greater among youths who have admitted to doing it; 62 percent of those who have plagiarized from the Internet consider it not serious.

A recent plagiarism controversy involving a German teenage writer, described in chapter 1, points to the presence of the free-for-all mindset among some young creators. In 2010, Helene Hegemann's critically acclaimed novel, *Axolotl Roadkill*, was poised to win a book prize when it was discovered to contain unattributed excerpts (including a full page of text) from another writer's novel and blog. Hegemann apologized and vowed to attribute all sources in a subsequent edition of the book. Yet she also justified her use of others' work by depicting herself as a member of a new generation of creators. In the words of Randy Kennedy, "she presented herself as a writer whose birthright is the remix, the use of anything at hand she feels suits her purposes, an idea of communal creativity that certainly wasn't shared by those from whom she borrowed."[22]

In public statements and interviews, Hegemann repeatedly said, "There's no such thing as originality anyway, just authenticity."[23] Author David Shields explicitly sought to make the same point about his contested novel, *Reality Hunger*, which is little more than a string of quotations from other writers. Both Shields and Hegemann are archetypes of what Kennedy calls "free-appropriation writers." Susan Blum's research with college students suggests that this attitude may be widespread; she observed that young people value sharing ideas over pursuing originality, which they see as difficult if not impossible to achieve.[24]

"Just for Fun": Comics and Other Playful Online Content

If we turn to other types of content—pictures, videos, and artwork—created for and appropriated in interest-based or hobbyist online communities, we also see evidence of multiple mindsets among youth. Relevant here is Jen Oxman Ryan's analysis of the attitudes and factors that shape tweens' approaches to a range of online appropriation situations, including "fun" activities such as participating in a comics Web site and accessing entertainment content online. Ryan found that at some point in their interviews, nearly all tweens conveyed a "copying is wrong" attitude consistent with intellectual property rights thinking. Yet attitudes such as "it's not a big deal," "it's not a copy," and "copying is normative online" were also expressed—particularly in relation to online content that is "playful" (i.e., not for school).[25]

Tweens' responses to a scenario about copying in a hypothetical online comics community are illustrative. We presented tweens with a scenario in which a newly posted comic contained a similar story line and identical phrases to an earlier comic posted on a comic creation Web site. When prompted, 64 percent of the youths said that the appropriation was "unfair" to the original comic author. Max, age 14, said, "Well, [even though] it's a public space, even though everything's available to see, I don't think you should copy someone else's work." Deva echoed, "It was their stuff and this person copied it."

Despite the fact that many youths perceived this act to be unfair, a substantial number (41 percent) would either ignore the violation or call attention to it only if it involved a friend whose content was being appropriated. Some tweens would decline to act because they "don't care," the infringement has no effect on them, or it is "not a big deal." Certainly, the decision to challenge a perceived injustice online can be fraught with tension, and for good reason; backlash might be expected to follow, especially if the challenge is made publicly. The trivializing attitude toward the injustice ("I don't care") is nevertheless noteworthy.

When asked if he would confront the situation, 11-year-old Anthony said, "There's nothing that big to do. It's not like—there's no copyright, I guess, there's no copyright sign. And they're allowed to copy it ... it's not like if they copy it, they get arrested. It's not that big of a deal. They copied it, but with a different ending. I wouldn't do anything."

Consistent with Anthony's attitude, nearly a third of tweens argued that the copying was acceptable. Tyler, age 12, argued that the copying was okay "because he's just copying the same thing, but having fun." Leticia, age 12, focused on the context for which the comic was created: "I wouldn't really do anything, because, personally, I don't like when people copy me, but that's only in school, or in work, or something. But not really on a Web site."

Related to this, when 10-year-old Cole was asked whether he thought people who contribute to such Web sites mind how their content is used, he replied, "No ... because it doesn't really matter. You don't get money for it." Beyond this specific scenario, 79 percent of the tweens trivialized similar instances of online appropriation, seeing them as "just not a big deal." And 36 percent suggested that copying, downloading, or reusing online content was expected and normative—or, as Ryan puts it, "modus operandi" online.[26] These ways of thinking suggest the presence of a free-for-all mindset in relation to Web content created for fun, in which rewards such as grades and money are not explicitly at stake.

This mindset may be appropriate in online communities with clear expectations that one's content can and will be appropriated and remixed in some way. However, even in those spaces, there can be disputes about how best to pay respect to the prior work of others. A study of youths who participate in Scratch, an online community that helps young people learn to build games and create pictures, provides relevant insights.

The researchers investigated how Scratch participants responded to having their work remixed. They focused on the youths' reactions to an automated attribution function on the site compared to instances in which remixers credited their sources manually or on their own. The researchers found that many youths perceived automated crediting to be less authentic, less meaningful, and even less moral than when a remixer went out of his or her way to give credit to the work.[27]

In our own study, we observed that the intellectual property mindset appeared with the greatest moral intensity when youths took the creator role and spoke, in either hypothetical or real terms, about others using their work. Here we found a clear "what's mine is mine" mindset. Recall that in the Wikipedia scenario, more than half of the youths perceived the content they had contributed to be theirs and were motivated to use it again in some fashion.[28]

Most youths in our study articulated that they expected others to respect their writings and other creative content by either attributing them or avoiding drawing on their work altogether. Sixty-five percent of the tweens said that they would object to someone copying their online content without attribution or in any form. Similarly, the teens and young adults conveyed the belief that their property should be protected; bloggers and other content creators were especially troubled by misappropriation of their writings, pictures, artwork, and videos. As William, a 20-year-old creator, said, "You don't want someone taking credit for your stuff."

The youths often articulated the belief that others shouldn't copy or fail to credit their work because of the time and effort the youths had invested, the personal meaning they attributed to their work, and the rewards (e.g., grades or praise) that they hoped to gain from it. Yet they also conveyed markedly less moral or ethical sensitivity about others' content, or even much reflection about its potential significance to the creators.

Rather, the nature of the content—and the young people's assumptions about its value—were more central than the assumed significance to the creators when deciding the acceptability of appropriating it. If the content appeared to be playful, funny, or of a category that is not valued in the larger society—such as a comic—it was often deemed to be "up for grabs." When the online content was of obvious *commercial* value, the youths frequently offered other, largely self-focused rationalizations for their use. Their typical approaches to music downloading are a clear case.

Getting and Sharing Music

Illegal downloading of music and film has been a highly contested yet widespread practice in the digital age, and youth have been central figures in it. College student Sean Parker's Napster platform was, in its heyday, perhaps the most well-known of what one of our teen interviewees referred to as a "bevy" of peer-to-peer sites for sharing and downloading music files. At its peak, Napster was reported to have had between 24 and 60 million users across the globe.[29]

Piracy on this scale placed pressure on the music and film industries, which fought back hard. Extensive litigation ultimately led to the demise of the original forms of sites like Napster and Limewire. iTunes and other pay-for-content sites have introduced relatively low-cost models that promise to monetize digital music and other content and thus temper industry concerns.[30] Nevertheless, piracy is still prevalent in the United States. A 2011 survey by the American Assembly found that 46 percent of all adult respondents and 70 percent of respondents ages 18–29 admitted that they had downloaded content illegally.[31]

The majority of the youths in our study reported actively engaging in illegal downloading or said they had done so in the past: 57 percent of the tweens and 93 percent of the teens and young adults told us that they had used sites such as BitTorrent, Hype Machine, Kazaa, Limewire, and MegaUpload to access copyrighted music, television shows, and movies without pay. However, such usage statistics tell us little about the ways of thinking and mindsets that youth bring to this practice.

As noted earlier in this chapter, the relationship between the legality of a practice and its ethical connotations is not straightforward. Internet activists often have cogent, ethically sensitive arguments in defense of piracy and other copyright violations.[32] Previous research indicates that motivations ranging from purely selfish to justice-oriented have been found among youth who engage in illegal appropriation of music and other artistic content.[33] When we spoke with the youths, we sought to uncover the extent to which their thinking revealed sensitivity and a sense of responsibility to the range of stakeholders implicated in downloading practices.[34] We also listened for the influence of peers and technological affordances in piracy-related decision making.

Although our most extensive conversations about music downloading were with the teens and young adults, comments from the tweens were also revealing. When asked about the kinds of sites they use to access music and videos, many tweens shared inaccurate information or conveyed confusion about whether the sites they used—and their specific uses of them—were legal. A lack of knowledge of copyright, or "copyright confusion," has been found among tweens in other studies as well.[35] The fact that some tweens access content with help from older siblings or parents contributes to this lack of knowledge.[36]

In contrast, most of the teens and young adults were well aware of the legality or, more often, the illegality of the sites they were using. They recognized when their practices constituted a violation of the legal property rights of musicians and record companies. How they thought about and justified such violations revealed the presence of both the "what's theirs is theirs" and the free-for-all mindsets about piracy, as well as different degrees of moral and ethical sensitivity.

Of the teens and young adults asked about downloading, 7 percent reported that they never obtained music or other content illegally, and 10 percent reported that they had done so in the past but had stopped. Among these youths, we saw the strongest evidence of the property rights mindset against downloading. Fifteen-year-old Abdul argued, "It seems like a whole cheating-the-system thing. Because you're basically cheating the company out of their money."

Elements of Abdul's mindset were also present among a larger group of the youths: 40 percent of the teens and young adults who actively pirated material suggested that their illegal downloading was perhaps unfairly taking profits away from musicians and record companies. Jared, age 24, said, "If you like a band and you want to support them, it's their thing that they're putting out there. You wouldn't want to not get paid for what you're putting out there." Young people like Jared realize that piracy may have a negative effect on musicians, yet as will be shown below, they often hold competing beliefs that justify or neutralize their decisions to download content without pay.[37]

As with the content creators in other appropriation scenarios, knowing the musicians personally or being a musician oneself affected the degree to which the youths exhibited moral sensitivity about piracy. Violet, age 18, shared, "I think it's better to just support the artists because, like I said, my boyfriend is studying music. Would I want his music being stolen? No, because he's the one that's going to have to pay for stuff."

Carlos, a 21-year-old budding musician who used to pirate all his music, told us about his change of heart: "I guess because I got more involved with music, more seriously involved with music, and I kind of started to learn about what illegal downloading—how that can affect and how that is currently affecting music careers, and how the music industry is suffering because of that. So I choose not to support it in that respect."

Nevertheless, other youths who have personal connections to the music world hold rather ambivalent, even half-hearted, positions on piracy. Eighteen-year-old Rosa's stance is illustrative:

Some of my friends are artists or upcoming artists. So I know they do this—they make their albums, obviously for their fans, but also it takes a lot of money to create them, so you get a lot of that money back by selling it. And that's pretty much their—like, if you work at Stop and Shop or something, you're getting a paycheck for what you're doing. If we buy a CD—that's their paycheck. So it's like, they're losing money. But I don't know. I kind of don't care at the same time.

Similarly, Michelle, age 17, shared, "It's their money, it's their music.... I wouldn't want anybody to leak my music if I was [a musician]. Because I know my brother gets upset when he sells a CD, and they burn it, and pass it on, pass it on, pass it on. So it kind of affects ... but I don't really think about it."

Both Rosa and Michelle are sensitive to the ways in which piracy may negatively affect musicians—family members and friends included. Yet at the same time they "don't care" or "don't really think about it" and download music anyway. In their thinking about piracy, they elevate other considerations. Rosa elaborates, "Sometimes you don't want to buy an entire album of a certain musician. You just want that one certain song. So I don't want to pay 13 bucks for just one song that I want to listen to." And Michelle minimizes the effects of her downloading "because I don't think me [sic] alone is making that much of a difference by downloading. When you think about it, everyone downloads."

Although these youths do display some moral sensitivity, it is ultimately overshadowed by indifference ("I kind of don't care"), self-focused thinking ("I don't want to pay 13 bucks"), or both. Moreover, their thinking represents a troubling disconnect between their actions and a larger trend that, by their own admission, may harm people they *do* care about.

Related to this, 87 percent of the teens and young adults offered self-focused or consequence-oriented rationales for illegal downloading. Financial reasons were cited most often (by 58 percent of these youths), followed by the low probability of being caught (45 percent), the convenience of obtaining content online (44 percent), and uncertainty about whether they would like the music, which made it "not worth it" to purchase (24 percent).

Serena, age 19, was motivated by financial reasons: "If you have the money for [iTunes], knock yourself out. If you're struggling to pay your tuition, I don't think you want to be spending a dollar per song." Madeline, age 21, was more concerned about convenience: "I'm not going to walk to Blockbuster and get it. I'm just going to spend two hours [downloading it].... That's easy to me. That's convenience, not taking 20 minutes to walk to Blockbuster and pay for it." Lam, age 21, put it even more succinctly, "I could pay the artist, I suppose, but it's not even just a matter of it being free; it's a matter of it just being so easy."

These ways of thinking suggest a blind spot regarding the moral and ethical issues that may be at play. Similarly, a study conducted by Shoshana Altschuller and Raquel Benbunan-Fich suggests that some youths' attitudes reveal a "total disregard" for the effect of their piracy on others.[38]

Twenty-nine percent of the youths in our study who downloaded content illegally *did* reflect on the effects on musicians and other artists, but they argued either that their piracy resulted in little or no harm or that they supported musicians in other ways (such as going to their concerts). Emma, age 20, said, "I guess [it doesn't matter] because I don't do it very often. I really want this song, I can't get it from anywhere else, it can't hurt. And in terms of supporting bands, they get all their money from concerts anyway; they don't get it from albums. I'm not trying to 'dis' the bands or anything. I don't think they're missing out." This "no harm done" perspective has been found to an even greater extent in other studies.[39]

Forty-six percent of the teens and young adults shared attitudes about getting and sharing music that cohere with a free-for-all mindset. Among nearly 60 percent of these youth, we found ethically sensitive critiques of the music and other entertainment industries from the perspective of consumers or artists. Most prevalent here were complaints that musicians, record companies, film studios, and even software companies have enough money and often overcharge for their products. Piracy, to these youths, is a way to narrow the gap between the "haves" and the "have-nots."

Sixteen year-old Will said, "I can't imagine how much money artists would be making if they also got the money that people are not spending on music. It'd be absurd." Alexis, age 25, argued that file sharing removes financial barriers that prevent low-income people from accessing music and other cultural goods. In her words, the practice "levels the playing ground" among consumers. Alexis's mindset might be more aptly called "free for good," since she sees open content as a way of creating a more equitable society.

Alexis, along with a handful of other youths, also argued that musicians were suffering under an unfair system of rewards: "Fairness [of piracy] doesn't even come into play, because the fact is, the people who are making money off those albums are [in] the record company. A lot of the time, the deals they make, an artist only gets like five cents [for] every album. That's bullshit."

We also observed a greater concern among many youths for piracy's effects on independent artists. Violet, age 18, said, "With independent artists—that's their money going out the window. If there is some famous, crazy pop star and they're making millions of dollars, they're not going to miss one song.... But I do listen to a lot of underground music, and I don't want to gyp [sic] those people of their money, because they're trying to make a living."

Asked whether she would buy music from big pop stars, Violet replied, "I would, I guess. I would prefer to just download it for free. I get burned CDs from friends and then I put those onto my computer." Youth like Violet apply the "what's theirs is theirs" mindset to certain creators—typically "indie" musicians—but draw on the free-for-all mindset for "pop stars." Similar concerns about the livelihood of independent artists and critiques of the profit structure of the music and entertainment industries have been voiced by youth in other studies.[40]

More than half of the youths who evinced a free-for-all mindset conveyed fatalistic arguments about the viability of the "old" model of the creative industries, given digital technologies and Internet culture. These youths suggested that piracy is normative today in youth culture, if not among the broader population.

Pedro, age 19, emphasized the role of technology: "It was bound to happen with the Internet. The easy way is to move files, which is the natural direction that technology is taking." Other youths, like Jared, pointed to the normative dimensions of downloading: "You don't really think about it, just because everyone's so accustomed to doing it now.... I think with just the way that the Internet is now and the accessibility to basically everything and anything you can basically want ... people will be able to share things online, regardless of how much you restrict it or not."

The belief that digital technologies encourage file sharing, that "everybody does it," and that it is therefore "unstoppable" were prominent among these youths, crystallizing a free-for-all mindset.

Thus, the youths' narratives about the controversial topic of illegal downloading revealed aspects of both the "what's theirs is theirs" and the free-for-all mindsets and often a back-and-forth dynamic between them. Morally and ethically sensitive ways of thinking are to be found in both mindsets, along with more self-focused concerns. However, as with other forms of appropriation, the youths were often more attuned to the consequences—potential rewards or sanctions—for themselves than they were to the moral or ethical dimensions of piracy. Tweens', teens', and young adults' top concerns about downloading were focused on computer viruses or getting in trouble with the law. Although ethically sensitive critiques of the music industry and related arguments in support of piracy exist and were engaged by some youths, most youths' downloading practices were guided by less virtuous aims.

Accounting for Property Blind Spots and Disconnects

My aim in this chapter has been to provide a nuanced portrait of how youth think about the various property scenarios that arise routinely in the digital age. I did this by referring to two opposing mindsets that youth embrace, and interchange, as they talk about the appropriation of others' and their own online content. At various points, I hinted at technological, cognitive, social, and cultural factors supporting youth's ways of thinking about the use of online content. Here I provide a brief discussion of these factors.

First is the critical question of how digital technologies contribute to the property disconnects and blind spots that are found too often among young people. As noted, digital media facilitate new levels of access to content and the capacity to seize and remix it for a variety of purposes. These relatively new affordances arguably contribute to an apparent ambivalence among some youths about whether creative content belongs to someone or should be free for all. The ease of access to music was often raised by youth as a key motivator for downloading it illegally; as one put it, "It's just so easy."

Adding to the ease is the reality that the connection between one's click to download content and its distant effects on others is often invisible. One study found high school and college students more accepting of using digital content without permission or payment than use of another's physical content.[41] This suggests a belief that the digital form is less valuable or capable of protection than other forms.[42] Studies that show that some youth, especially those who plagiarize online content, dismiss the seriousness of digital cheating are relevant here, too.[43]

Nevertheless, we should avoid concluding that the technologies are *causing* property-related blind spots and disconnects. Although digital affordances lay the foundation for what we can do, individual, social, and cultural factors interact with these opportunities in powerful ways, influencing how youth, and all of us, seize them.

Certainly there are developmental as well as individual factors that contribute to youth's mindsets about property. Our study suggests that tweens
do not have a sophisticated understanding of the legality of certain Web
sites. Their understanding of copyright is vague at best; a little less than
half said that they did not know what the term meant, and less than a
quarter had never even heard the term before.[44] The term *copyright confusion* is often used to describe this common finding among youth. However,
Renee Hobbs suggests that the problem is hardly confined to youth; educators frequently exhibit uncertainty about what is legal versus illegal use of
others' material.[45]

Nevertheless, given the likely gaps between the legal and the ethical, youth's understanding of what it means to comply with rather than
infringe on copyright law is not a sufficient goal. Cultivating sensitivity
to the dilemmas, and then the capacity and inclination to understand the
human effects of appropriation choices, is more vital. Also essential is the
capacity to grasp the problematic dimensions and ethical significance of
intellectual property law and the creative industries' efforts to protect their
content. A sophisticated understanding of the complex issues at play may
be too much to expect of youth, especially children and tweens. However,
as shown by some of our study participants, teens and young adults can
often grasp the fundamental issues at stake; whether they do so depends on
their sensitivity to the dilemmas, their motivation to consider them fully,
and the availability of support.

Individual factors also play a role. The beliefs and values of youth and
their experiences with creator roles shape their moral and ethical sensitivity
to property situations. Some youths talked about "having a conscience" in
relation to the use of others' material, but others conveyed rather laissez-
faire attitudes, blind spots, and disconnects. Another study showed that
youths who exhibit a tolerance of unethical or illegal conduct in general are
more likely to engage in piracy than youths who do not have this generic
tolerance.[46]

Turning to the influence of assuming creative roles, we saw that bloggers emphasized giving credit to others in their writings. Some musicians
or friends of musicians had more scruples about piracy than nonmusi-
cians, but this was not always the case. As we saw, some youths revealed
half-hearted and ultimately self-focused positions about piracy regardless
of their personal connections. In fact, very few of the young people we

interviewed put forth ethically sensitive arguments about freedom of information and other content akin to the beliefs held by the late Aaron Swartz.

Without a doubt, peers, adults, and messages from the broader society powerfully influence the mindsets that youth adopt about plagiarism and other forms of appropriation. "Everybody does it" was a common refrain from the teens and young adults we interviewed about illegal music downloading. Self-focused, as opposed to ethical, rationales for piracy also appeared to be normative. In terms of the appropriation of text, the youths in our study often alluded to peers who inappropriately use online content for their papers. Other studies have shown that cheating behavior is heavily influenced by real or perceived cheating by peers.[47] Moreover, the larger backdrop of academic pressure from parents and fierce competition for admission to top colleges and high-status jobs has been widely discussed—especially given recent cheating scandals at top secondary schools and colleges.[48]

The Word from Adults: What Youth Hear about Online Property Issues

Despite the propensity of youth to rebel against adults, the conduct of parents and teachers and their messages to youth can have enormous effects. Consider the likely effect on youth of educators who take a largely penal approach to discouraging plagiarism versus discussing the moral and ethical significance of attribution. It is clear that a greater emphasis on penal approaches—combined with the use of plagiarism-checking Web sites such as Turnitin—is contributing to the consequence-oriented stances of most youths in our study. They frequently mentioned the weighty consequences that await students who are caught plagiarizing. In contrast, educators who emphasize the value of giving credit to a creator's ideas and influence (rather than threatening with a failing grade) are better poised to cultivate ethical sensitivity to these issues—and thus a more reliable and meaningful basis for respecting others' creative work.

Adults may also be unwitting antimentors. Many adults lack familiarity with interest-based communities for playful online content and gaming worlds and may therefore make light of the appropriation of others' content in such spaces. Parents and other influential adults may also encourage consequence-oriented ways of thinking about piracy. Among the teens and young adults we interviewed, nearly one-third reported that an adult in their lives had encouraged piracy in some way: by engaging in it themselves, by helping youths do it, or by turning to youths for advice about illegal downloading.

One college student described how a professor helped her download a software program and skirt the licensing issue. As noted, piracy can be accompanied by ethically sensitive ways of thinking, but none of these youths reported that the adults in their lives held or shared ethical stances about downloading. More typical was this comment from 15-year-old Trey: "My mom is all for [downloading], because she thinks it's absolutely asinine to pay $35 for a DVD or $65 for a game or $100 to $250 for an operating system." One-third of the parents and teachers with whom we spoke reported engaging in piracy, and only one of them shared an ethically sensitive argument for the practice.

Overall, adult messages appear to do much to encourage consequence-oriented stances and little to cultivate moral and ethical ways of thinking about appropriation in the digital age. We found significant evidence of a mentorship gap. Our data suggest that adults rarely delve into the moral, ethical, or legal complexity of property issues in their conversations with youth. Our interviews with educators indicated that some of them did not feel knowledgeable enough to have in-depth conversations with youth about copyright and related issues. Other teachers felt equipped to facilitate these discussions but did not engage in them, probably due to limited time in the school day.

Conclusion

In facilitating access to original works that can be used in new and exciting but also outright derivative ways, the Internet raises new dilemmas—or at least heightens the salience of old ones. The landscape is certainly complex. On the one hand, creators may well have a moral basis for expecting attribution, payment, or other forms of acknowledgment of their work. On the other hand, systems that protect content creators and owners may well be unethical if they unfairly inhibit creativity and public access to content and information.

This complicated state of affairs has inspired technological innovations, thoughtful dialogue, and even movements focused on creating a more just system, but the issues are not easily resolved. In this period of flux, it is critical for youth to be sensitive to, and ideally take part in dialogue about, the ethical dimensions of property and credit issues, even if there is uncertainty about the ethical status of their practices. However, they need support from adults in order to do so.

We observed evidence among youth of both an intellectual property mindset and a free-for-all mindset. In both of these mindsets, however, youth exhibit less sensitivity to the moral and ethical issues than one might hope. Although we found general agreement that attributing, and not plagiarizing, others' words and ideas is important, the ethical underpinnings of citation are not foremost in youth's minds (unless they are thinking about their own work).

As we looked at other types of content, especially music, we saw that the youths presented a series of justifications for illegal appropriation. And even though ethical concerns appeared, they were far less prominent than self-focused justifications for piracy.

The data presented here point to some troubling disconnects and blind spots about the ethics of appropriation among youth. However, the conclusion is not that most "kids these days" are simply immoral or unethical. Given the complex environments—social, cultural, and technological—in which youth are immersed, self-centered approaches to the appropriation scenarios discussed here may make sense.

Therefore, in considering ways to reconnect the disconnects and correct the blind spots, we should be taking a hard look at key influences—including, and perhaps especially, the roles of adults. It is crucial to consider the ineffective, if not deeply problematic, messages about the dos and don'ts of appropriation conveyed by educators, parents, and other influential figures in youth's lives.

Specifically, conversations about attribution in schoolwork should shift from an emphasis on punishment to a discussion of the ethical dimensions of citation. Taking on the roles of creators or at least routinely taking creator perspectives may go a long way in cultivating greater sensitivity to the dilemmas in play.[49] Similarly, discussions about downloading music and other content should ideally involve broader considerations than the legality or illegality of one's download.

In general, we need a balanced approach that empowers youth to seize the positive opportunities of digital media for creativity and knowledge building while instilling ethical sensitivity. Youth need better education not just about how to create, attribute, respect, and draw on others work but also about *why* it is important to do so.

4 Participation

To Scam or Not to Scam: A Gamer's Dilemma

For the past two weeks, you have been playing an online multiplayer game that has about 30,000 members and takes place in a 3-D world. Yesterday you joined a club within the game. Your fellow club members, none of whom you know offline, seem very nice and have already given you lots of game advice as well as some useful equipment for your character.

Buying, selling, and trading such equipment with other players is a fun and important part of the game, but there are few rules about trading, and exchanges don't always end well for some players. You've noticed, for example, that many of your clubmates brag to one another about taking advantage of new players by selling them worthless green rocks, called *pseudogems*, for very high prices. After finding some pseudogems while doing a joint quest with two of your clubmates, you are invited by one of them to travel to a nearby town to try to sell the pseudogems to inexperienced players for a big profit. Would you go with your clubmates to the nearby town to sell the pseudogems?

Even if you've never played a massive multiplayer online game (MMOG) such as *EverQuest, RuneScape,* or *World of Warcraft,* you can probably grasp the key features of this scenario and its dilemma: to scam or not to scam new players.

Even so, for the nongamers out there, let me call attention to certain qualities of MMOGs that are relevant here. First, as the term *massive* suggests, the scale of many of these games is considerable. Some games have been reported to have more than 10 million subscribers.[1] Second, these games are deeply social. Collaboration with other players and membership in groups or guilds is often a core element of the game. Third, these games constitute persistent worlds. The choices players make stick with their characters, or avatars, for as long as they participate in the game—sort of like real life.[2]

These qualities exist as points of departure from other kinds of games: board games, card games, and traditional video games in which one's opponent is the computer and one game is typically limited to one encounter. Indeed, these qualities may make such games more similar to online communities built around other purposes, such as social networking, fandom, and cocreation.

But how should participants conceive of these spaces: as merely games or as communities in which participants have moral and ethical responsibilities? These kinds of questions have been a frequent topic of discussion among both players and scholars of video games. Some suggest that video games, even those of the MMOG variety, are play spaces set apart from real life in which alternate codes of conduct apply.[3]

This perspective finds support in Johan Huizinga's classic play theory, which presents games as "magic circles" in which moral concerns may be suspended.[4] Along these lines, some scholars and gamers argue that video games provide safe spaces to experiment with being a "bad guy" without concern for real consequences and therefore with no moral regret.[5] However, others balk at the notion that actions taken in games, particularly MMOGs, have no consequences and that there is any benefit from being able to be a "bad guy" without experiencing moral regret.

Dorothy Warner and Mike Raiter describe MMOGs as complex "social structures" that raise "ethical questions regarding players' personal responsibility, behavior, and expectations of each other, as well as how conflict is managed."[6] Controversies have erupted in MMOGs in response to a range of actions, including sexual harassment and mass fraud of fellow players.[7]

Complaints about and efforts to stem "griefing" (purposely harassing or killing another player simply for fun) and other forms of "toxicity" are widespread in these contexts.[8] Players on the receiving end of such acts experience losses of in-game currency and the time they invested accruing it and achieving a given level in the game. These factors suggest that the moral and ethical significance of in-game actions cannot easily be dismissed. However, the extent to which they are is up to the participants.

"Sell the Gems": Youths Respond

We posed the scenario above to 27 teens and young adults (including both gamers and nongamers) in order to gauge the extent to which they perceived action in such contexts to have moral or ethical dimensions. When asked if they would scam innocent new players in a MMOG by selling them worthless pseudogems, nearly half of the respondents replied that they would sell the gems, almost a quarter would sell them in certain kinds of games but not others, and just over a quarter would not sell them regardless of the context. However, more significant than the decision to sell or not sell was the reasoning offered by the youths.[9]

The most common response to this scenario was that "it's just a game." More than half of the young people to whom we presented this dilemma shared something along the lines of 21-year-old Melissa's thinking: "There's nothing wrong with taking advantage of new people playing a video game, because it's a video game. It's not real life." The frequency with which this response appeared suggests that despite the qualities that make MMOGs seem real, many youth are reluctant to conceive of them as more than simply games.

Twenty-year-old Christina elaborated, "Well, in real life, I'd love to do this and get away with it, but if you have any morals or have half a conscience, you'd know that you just couldn't do that to a friend. But online, you can throw all those morals and that conscience to the wind." Alexis, age 25, summed up this stance well when she said, "The dilemma kind of is removed. There are no morals to be considered there."

Thus, among nearly a quarter of the youths, we observed the belief that unethical conduct is expected and justifiable in games because games are competitive by nature. These youths argued that the aim of a game is to win, which means that creative strategies are part of the game even when technically prohibited by the rules.

This conception of games as spaces in which anything goes was not shared by all youths, however. A little more than half of the teens and young adults we asked about the dilemma showed at least some sensitivity to its moral or ethical dimensions. Some of these youths reported they would sell the pseudogems but might feel some moral regret, especially if they came to know the players they scammed.

Nora, age 19, reflected, "I guess if I had a relationship with the player ... if I knew them or if I started talking to them and they were nice or something, I'd probably feel pretty bad about it." Other youths evinced more committed moral stances. For instance, Miley, age 16, said, "I wouldn't take advantage of somebody that doesn't know what the deal is, what's going on or how things work.... It's not fair to them. I mean, it's just being mean, I guess."

The thinking here is focused on the principles of fairness and kindness, rather than meanness, that Miley believes should guide interactions with others. In other words, "play nice." Similarly, 15-year-old Margot considered the perspectives of the new players: "I think that if I was new, I wouldn't want that to happen to me." She invoked the Golden Rule, "Do unto others as you would want them to do unto you," as a guide for her response.

A small number of youths considered the wider implications of selling pseudogems for the integrity of the game and its community of players. Sarah, age 23, responded, "I would tell my friends I was going to tell [the new players that the gems are worthless], and I would say, 'Listen, like, we're all in this society together, but I think you're really not promoting a good, fair game. And what's the point in your gain if you cheated your way to it?'"

Julian, age 23, more explicitly considers the game community in his response: "If everyone begins to feel cheated, then it can have an impact on the community sense and community feel of the game." The "it's a community" approach of Sarah and Julian contrasts sharply with the "it's just a game" stance found among more teens and young adults in response to this scenario.

Overall, this game context scenario revealed a few distinct approaches to MMOGs. Some youth exhibited sensitivity to the moral and ethical dimensions of games that engage large numbers of people in a persistent virtual world. Attention to fairness and the Golden Rule as well as the mindset that MMOGs are communities surfaced among these youth. However, the more common attitude was that actions taken in a game context have little or no moral significance—that is, "it's just a game."

MMOGs are contexts in which many of the unique qualities of digital environments—interactivity, anonymity, scalability, and distance—are prominently featured. Thus, attitudes toward such games can provide a useful starting point for considering the broader question of how we engage with and treat one another in other virtual spaces that share some of those key qualities. Without the "magic circle" that marks online games as play spaces, do we approach nongame online spaces with greater moral and ethical sensitivity? To what extent do we harbor the belief that what happens on sites like Facebook, Twitter, Reddit, and Tumblr is not real or is less real than face-to-face interactions in the physical world, and how do such beliefs affect our actions?

In what follows, I consider selected participation dilemmas that we face as we engage in online communities of various sorts. I then turn to further data about the mindsets—including the blind spots and disconnects—that the youths in our study brought to some of these dilemmas and what those mindsets suggest about the integrity of the communities being forged on the Internet. As in the other chapters, I also consider *why* the youths display more or less ethical sensitivity to these issues—the developmental, social, cultural, and technological forces that, to various degrees, influence their mindsets and choices.

Online Participation: The Dilemmas

The theme of this chapter, participation, is considerably broader than the other two themes addressed in this book. The *Oxford English Dictionary* defines *participation* as "the action of taking part in something." Merriam-Webster's definition includes a further element: "the state of being related to a larger whole." Considered together, these definitions point to two key dimensions of participation: individual agency and connection to a larger entity.

These dimensions are not always in harmony, however. The tension between the individual and society is a persistent feature of human social life.[10] How that tension plays out as we take part in digital environments with their unique qualities is the key concern of this chapter. I treat participation broadly as the nature of one's conduct on the Web and, as in the other chapters, explore the extent to which that conduct is morally and ethically sensitive. That is, to what extent do our habits of connectivity coincide with an inclination to pursue our own agendas rather than increase our sensitivity to the perspectives of others and our attachment to communities? To what extent do we treat the Internet as *my* space versus *our* space?

Questions along these lines have inspired both optimistic and pessimistic perspectives. Optimists, including Henry Jenkins and Clay Shirky, cite the opportunities to connect with others, to be exposed to diverse perspectives, and to form "participatory cultures" and other communities around social, civic, and political interests as key affordances of the Web.[11] Jane McGonigal is an enthusiastic proponent of video games as generative spaces for considering and testing solutions to real-world problems.[12]

Yet critics, including Andrew Keen and Sherry Turkle, argue that digital technologies, social media, and the ways in which we use them ultimately isolate and divide us, diminish our relationships, and perhaps even encourage narcissism.[13] Whether the Internet fulfills utopian dreams or dystopian nightmares, or a mix of the two, depends on our choices, of course.[14] How we conduct ourselves, treat one another, and contribute to the rich reservoir of online content ultimately determines the goodness of the Internet.

There are numerous entry points for exploring these big questions about online conduct. The concept of participation is arguably broad enough to encompass the issues addressed in both the privacy and the property chapters. Below, I point to a handful of participatory practices that highlight tensions between individual and collective interests online and that sometimes reveal disconcerting ethical blind spots and disconnects.

Gaming the Internet
The multiplayer game scenario above explored how youth think about the ethics of participation, pitting the agenda of an individual and a small group against fair treatment of others and the integrity of a larger community. Related questions can be posed about the ethics of participation in other online contexts that can hardly be considered play spaces. One can find numerous cases in which individuals have sought to "game" online communities and search engines for personal gain.

Google Places, a participatory, or Web 2.0, version of the Yellow Pages, came under fire recently after business owners complained that their establishments were erroneously listed as closed. The site contains a feature whereby users can simply click a button to tag a business as "reportedly closed" or, if enough people click it, "permanently closed"—a status that proves difficult to reverse. Aggrieved business owners contend that the feature is being abused by dissatisfied customers or malicious competitors seeking to hinder their businesses.[15] In a stunt designed to push back on

Google's lax oversight of this feature, a technology blogger recently subjected the search engine company to a taste of its own medicine. After he and just one friend submitted "closed" reports on Google's own business listing for its Mountain View, California, headquarters, the office was automatically tagged as "reportedly closed."[16]

Similar concerns have arisen on Yelp, another online business directory where users can rate and comment on restaurants, hair salons, and even auto mechanics. Some business owners have allegedly paid people for high ratings and glowing comments here.[17] Amazon is no stranger to these practices, either. In September 2012, popular crime novelist R. J. Ellory was accused of "sock-puppeting," or posting favorable reviews of his own work and negative reviews of other novelists' works anonymously on Amazon. Ellory is just the most recent case of abuse involving the anonymous review feature on the world's largest retail Web site.[18]

These cases raise questions about how we approach the opportunities and consider our responsibilities as we take part, anonymously or otherwise, in Web 2.0. If we participate in "crowd sourcing"—sharing information, praise, or concerns about a business, health topic, or public issue—do we do so constructively and authentically? When using the Internet to advertise a business or an organization or to promote our ideas, do we act with a sense of fairness even while pursuing our interests in profit, status, and other rewards? These dilemmas concern how our actions affect the integrity of online communities—the extent to which these communities can be trusted and whether they contribute to or detract from the public good.

Online Speech

If we think of *speech* in the broadest possible way, all the content that exists on the Web can be considered a form of speech. The Internet is made up of a rich supply of text, video, audio, and imagery, replenished on an ongoing basis as we are perpetually invited to upload, update, comment, and tweet. And we can readily forward, "like," and retweet content posted by others, with or without our own commentary. With few editors mediating our access to the public sphere, we can lend our voices to and take part in communities ranging from friends-only groups to a vast public.

The capacity for unrestrained speech may be the most celebrated feature of the Web, and it is frequently defended even when the speech in question is wounding, hateful, threatening, or able to be interpreted as such.[19]

As discussed in the privacy chapter, online content is scalable—it has the potential to "go viral" or be shared with a larger public than intended or even imagined. Given this quality, our online speech is potentially high stakes and poised to affect others in ways that are beyond our control once the speech is posted. Elisabeth Soep thus warns of the uncertain "digital afterlives" of our online expressions.[20]

Picture Problems, Text Trouble

Given the possibility of eternal digital life, how we take up the Web's invitations to upload and share photos and videos is significant. Do we upload impulsively or even, as with Instagram, automatically? Or do we "think before [we] post?"[21] Cautionary tales of ill-considered uploads and text messages abound—including by some public officials who, when outed, faced potentially career-ending scrutiny.

Further complicating the question of the things we post is that even fairly innocuous content is open to an array of interpretations far from the intentions of the poster. A frequent stumbling block in digital communication is the fact that all online content can be taken out of context and thus stripped of its intended meaning, whether that be irony, sarcasm, or a political statement. This problem is not particular to digital media, but it is exacerbated by them, given the ease with which we can copy, paste, forward, and share content *without* contextual or authorial information relevant for interpretation.

With text, we face the additional burden of the absence of tone. In accordance with J. L. Austin's speech act theory, the deeper meaning behind our words—the *illocutionary* dimension—can be lost when facial cues and intonation are absent. The intended effect on our audiences—the *perlocutionary* dimension—is therefore vulnerable.[22] The use of emoticons (e.g., ☺), abbreviations (e.g., LOL, J/K), and other cues of intended tone and meaning can certainly help mitigate misinterpretations, but these markers are far from foolproof.[23]

Complicating things further, online speakers can embed hidden meanings for specific audiences in their status updates, tweets, and comments.[24] Related to this are the practices of "subtweeting" or "vaguebooking," the use of tweets and Facebook status updates to indicate an unspecified crisis or to express anger at an unidentified target; such posts are widely viewed as schemes to gain attention from followers and friends.[25]

Regardless of the cues we include in our online speech, there will always be an interpretive gap: a distance between our intended meaning and the range of meanings that known and unknown others may perceive. Given this reality, pausing before we post to consider how our words may be read and (mis)interpreted by countless others, both known and unknown to us, seems prudent. It's far from clear that thinking before we post is routine, however.

Disagreeable Dialogue

If we consider the array of rich opportunities for dialogue about social and political issues online, we are confronted with further dilemmas about how we express our ideas and opinions, especially contrarian views. This issue may be particularly salient when we join discussions anonymously; a recent study showed that comments on Facebook, where participants are identifiable, are more civil than comments posted in spaces where anonymity is the norm.[26] If our offline identities are disconnected from our words, and we are dialoguing from behind a screen, we might not be as civil and respectful as we would in a face-to-face conversation. How we balance the opportunities for voice with the possibility that our speech can be uncivil, harmful, or misinterpreted as such is a key challenge.

These questions are even more germane in contexts where hostile speech is arguably normative—for example, the comments section of a CNN.com or *Huffington Post* article or following even the most benign YouTube video. In the early days of the Internet, terms such as *flaming* and *trolling* arose to describe aggressive, usually anonymous, online speech that persists today in online forums, news, and content sharing sites.[27] Some research suggests that participants in such settings frequently adopt the tone of other participants; in other words, flaming breeds flaming online.[28]

Similarly, respectful or kind speech should breed more of the same. Although many online communities are marked by respectful, supportive, and even caring dynamics, the perception that incivility and disrespect are rampant, if not normative, on the Internet is commonplace.[29] Recent steps taken by the *Huffington Post* to disallow anonymous participation and by *Popular Science* to close comments altogether may be one way to deal with this. However, such steps may also reduce opportunities for voice and undercut authentic dialogue about sensitive topics.[30]

Cruel Content

Turning to nonanonymous online settings, we might expect to see consistently respectful discourse among people who are typically known to one another offline. However, studies suggest a mixed picture. A 2011 Pew study of the tenor of dialogue on social network sites found 85 percent of adults reporting "mostly kind" interactions and positive experiences.

A study of teens by Pew conducted the same year had less heartening results. Compared with adults, teens had more frequent exposure to online cruelty. When the teens in Pew's focus groups were asked to describe how people usually act online, the responses most frequently included the words *mean, rude,* and *disrespectful.*[31]

A 2011 Associated Press–MTV survey found that 56 percent of the youths reported having experienced verbal abuse through social media, and a Common Sense Media survey found more than 40 percent of teens stating that they often or sometimes observe sexist, antigay, or racist comments online.[32]

Finally, a 2013 survey of adults ages 18 and older found that 78 percent of the respondents reported "rising incivility" and rudeness on sites such as Facebook and Twitter, some of which resulted in conflicts between family members and offline friends.[33]

Such intentional forms of online cruelty—variously described as *cyberbullying, digital abuse,* and *drama*—are thus a growing concern among youth. Digital avenues for expressing meanness are numerous and include posting embarrassing photos or videos of someone, making overtly mean comments on others' photos or "walls," and setting up social media profiles in order to mock or bully an individual.

Because of the potentially vast audience for any content posted online, a hateful comment about an individual—particularly one that targets his or her sex, race, sexual orientation, or other personal characteristic—can have implications both for the group to which he or she belongs and for the wider public. Individuals who identify with or are part of the group of the person being attacked may experience the slur personally. The sting of a misogynist attack may be felt by all female viewers even when it is originally aimed at a particular female blogger or gamer.

Moreover, online hate may convey to all viewers that such speech is appropriate or acceptable in such spaces, and (as flaming breeds flaming) it possibly encourages further cruelty. Therefore, in addition to dilemmas about what we post of our own, we face dilemmas about how to respond to the content we observe, especially what is posted by our friends and those whom we follow on Twitter, Instagram, or Tumblr.

What do we observe but then dismiss and ignore? The opportunities for by-standing in the face of uncivil, disrespectful discourse and even outright cruelty, bullying, or hate speech seem endless on the Web. Addressing such harm requires a wider sense of responsibility, both for distant others and for the moral climate of the communities that our actions and our inaction help to forge online.

What's the Norm?

Some of us might consider the ethics of our participation on the Internet mainly in light of our internal moral beliefs and values, such as a commitment to treating others with kindness and respect and confronting cruelty when we see it. Perhaps our actions are also informed by external policies set by our employers, our schools, or the social media sites themselves. However, much online conduct has a more powerful, albeit informal, base: norms.

The conduct of our friends and followers—including the content of their posted photos, comments, tweets, and other speech acts—signals to us what is acceptable or "fair game" online. In turn, what we actively post, what we observe but passively ignore, and what we push back on also set norms for our fellow participants. The normative boundaries of the Web are actively negotiated on an ongoing basis; we take part in the construction of the goodness of the Internet. However, the extent to which we think about the *normative* dimensions of what we and others do online is less clear.

Participation—considered here as the nature of our conduct online—is a broad enough term to capture pretty much anything we do online. I have limited this discussion to a handful of exemplary topics: crowd sourcing, photo and video posting, and other speech acts, with an emphasis on troubling cases. These topics reveal the participatory opportunities the Internet provides and demonstrate how our actions can have indelible connections to large public networks, whether we acknowledge it or not. Digital qualities such as anonymity and the distance between ourselves and others online can be seized in ways that (intentionally or not) taint the moral and ethical character of online communities, thus diminishing the promise of the Internet.

Turning back to our focus on youth, we need to consider the extent to which they are mindful of these kinds of dilemmas as they participate in social media sites and connect with one another, often around the clock, through their digital devices. Where and when do we see signs of conscientious connectivity rather than distanced, removed stances? In what follows, I focus my attention on youth perspectives on the ethics of posting and responding to negative speech and other content on the Web, revealing distinct and competing mindsets about the ethics of participation in digital contexts.

Participation on the Web: Youth Perspectives

When we begin to look deeply at how youth think about their participation on the Internet, there's one key idea to put on the table first: at this juncture—more than 20 years into the digital age—many youths feel little choice about *whether* to take part in Facebook, Twitter, Instagram, and other social media platforms. As with other long-standing social activities, such as going to parties, listening to popular music, and conforming to fashion trends, both subtle and blatant pressures make youth believe that their participation on social media sites is necessary and not optional.

In a 2013 study conducted by Pew and the Berkman Center for Internet and Society, many youths reported feeling socially compelled to use Facebook, even if it led to negative feelings about themselves or involvement in online "drama" that was acknowledged to be unproductive and even detrimental.[34] The 24/7, or "always on," quality of the Internet can exacerbate the pressure to participate on an ongoing basis to avoid missing out.

However, like other long-standing youth activities, online participation is not simply the result of peer pressure; tweens, teens, and emerging adults are engrossed in crucial phases of identity development, and the Internet can provide support even while it poses challenges. Media scholars recognized from the earliest days of the Internet that it offered new spaces in which to explore, express, and find support for one's identity, along with the option of doing so anonymously.[35]

On today's Internet, anonymity is hardly guaranteed, but venues for identity play persist for those who wish to take them up.[36] Similar to the findings of other research, our study found that youth seized opportunities to explore, reflect on, and express their developing identities to friends,

friends of friends, and even unknown people through online games, social network profiles, blogs, and instant messaging or chat programs.[37]

From around 2005 to 2009, when sites like Facebook largely engaged youth, these spaces had the added benefit of freedom from adults. Sherry Turkle notably described online spaces as new avenues for the "psychosocial moratoria" that psychologist Erik Erikson argued was crucial for developing a coherent sense of identity.[38] Given the recent colonization of Facebook in particular by parents, teachers, and other adults, youth have become inventive at finding new ways of communicating with one another "below the radar" of adults; danah boyd has written about such strategies. Some youths have also migrated to alternate sites (e.g., Instagram and Tumblr) while maintaining a presence on Facebook—though not always happily.[39]

These data suggest that although many young people feel obligated to participate in online life, they also enjoy leveraging its affordances for their emerging identities and social relationships. When speaking about digital life in general, nearly all the youths in our study articulated both rich promises and worrying perils—for example, the Internet was described as connecting human beings but also disconnecting us physically as our interactions are increasingly mediated by screens. Overall, young people's perspectives on online participation are often double-edged, acknowledging both the virtues and the vices of mediated interactions.

Given these rather nuanced and ambivalent perceptions, it is important to explore how youths approach their own and others' online conduct, especially that which is troubling. Below, I explore the mindsets youths bring to the opportunities to express themselves on the Web, and the ways in which they respond to other people's expressions.

The Mindsets

In keeping with the ambivalence noted above, youth appear to be of multiple minds about the ethics of participation on the Internet. Looking at the youths' narratives about online speech in particular, I discerned the presence of three key mindsets informing their online decision making to various degrees. The first two mindsets, "play nice" and "it's a community," reflect attention to moral and ethical concerns, respectively. By contrast, the "it's just the Internet" stance is tied to a tendency to dismiss the moral and ethical gravity of pretty much anything that is posted online.

"Play Nice"

In young people of all ages, moral sensitivity is quite well developed and frequently voiced. As I framed it in chapter 1, moral thinking is marked by a concern for known others, often displayed through empathy and principles such as the Golden Rule ("Do unto others as you would have them do unto you") and its Internet variant ("Do unto others online as you would do unto them face-to-face"). The "play nice" mindset in relation to troubling online speech thus focuses on the emotional experiences of friends, peers, and other known targets of such speech.

The "play nice" stance was often displayed when the youths were asked about troubling comments, wall posts, or content that they had received or observed online. Just over half of the teens and young adults showed moral sensitivity in a similar manner to Madeline, age 21:

> I haven't had any negative comments, but things that I've seen that are negative that would make me feel bad is if someone commented about how I look in a negative light. I feel like if you don't have anything to say that's good, don't say anything at all. Kind of like the same rule as in life.... I don't think it's appropriate to say someone's ugly or fat or make a comment about their race.... I think that would really bum me out if someone called me a butter face or something on the Internet.... I think that would stand out to me a lot more than the hundreds of comments of people saying you're hot. It would hurt, definitely.

Madeline both takes the perspective of people who have received hurtful comments and invokes a moral rule centered on kindness. Trey, age 15, also points to moral principles as a guide for using sites likes Facebook:

> I think of it as you talk to someone on Facebook as you would talk to them in person. And same thing online. You don't treat someone like a jerk because you're behind the microphone.... Some people use [social network sites] as an attack system, just to attack people and then cower away because they can't do it in real life. I think it was last year, there was a girl and then someone used Facebook to attack her and ... just write a ton of things on Facebook like groups and comments.... Obviously, like you don't harass verbally someone through Facebook.... It's just like a real person. Would you say a racist comment to someone in real life or would you say it to them through Facebook? What's the difference?

In reflecting on online cruelty, sexism, and racism, Trey points to the distance between ourselves and others online—the fact that we text, post, and upload from behind a screen or a "microphone"—as a contributing factor, though not an excusable one.

We heard similar concerns from tweens. Ben, age 11, referred to the "confidence level" that mediated communication can impart, making it easier to type and then send a cruel text message: "I've seen [texting] cause trouble a few times ... the confidence level, that person probably made a mistake and would never say that in person, but they said it through a text ... [something like], 'You're ugly,' 'I hate you.' Something really mean and hurtful that you really wouldn't say to someone's face."

Forty-five percent of the tweens in our study reported seeing, or being involved in, similar conflicts in texts, instant messages, or Facebook comments and photos. Most of these youths expressed moral concerns about the effects of these actions on their friends and sometimes shared that their own feelings were hurt by cruel speech. Similarly, when we prompted this younger age group with a case of online hate directed at a teacher, just over one-quarter reacted that such speech was "mean," "rude," and "disrespectful."

The "play nice" mindset doesn't just surface in relation to situations youths have observed. Among a good number of them, empathy and Golden Rule thinking routinely inform their decisions about what to share online. In talking about the comments she posts on Facebook, 18-year-old Rosa shared, "I don't want to say something that would probably make them uncomfortable, seeing that other people would be able to see, or leaving an inappropriate comment or something. So I'll just leave it, but just make sure that it's something that's decent to read, not anything that would be bad, or cause bad reactions."

Like Rosa, just over half of the youths spoke about being mindful of the person on the receiving end of an online comment, photo, or video. These youths were conscious both of the distance between themselves and others in mediated communication and of the need to be guided by empathetic principles.

Similarly, when we asked tweens how they decide what to post about themselves and others on social networks, more than three-quarters suggested that they consider moral concerns in some way. Many of these youths talked about pausing and reflecting about hurt feelings that could result from posting a given comment or photo on Facebook. For example, 13-year-old Shonelle told us, "I would write something first and look back and read it over, make sure something is not a hurtful or bad thing."

Some youths reported that they avoid posting about other people entirely in order to sidestep potential harm—especially because of the interpretive gap online. Kiara, age 13, said, "I don't really post stuff about other people, because they could take it the wrong way." Concerns about upsetting or betraying close friends through revealing online photos and stories came up among almost one-third of the tweens, some of whom check with friends before posting content that features them. One check for their online conduct was to post only comments that they would actually say to the person face-to-face.

The prevalence of the "play nice" mindset among youths of all ages was heartening. Moral sensitivity is arguably necessary for the development of socially positive online interactions and communities. Thus, pausing to reflect on other people's feelings should be an essential routine before posting content online—especially given the frequently cited opportunities for the misinterpretation of online words. Nevertheless, given that Internet-based interactions often occur in public networks, where our speech can affect people whom we don't know personally, the "play nice" mindset is not entirely sufficient for the creation of ethical communities. Here is where the "it's a community" mindset comes in.

"It's a Community"

The "it's a community" mindset reflects ethical sensitivity—it involves recognition of the relationship between individuals' online actions and the tone and integrity of online communities. Here I explore how this mindset appears when young people consider troubling speech acts, such as negative comments, bullying, and hate speech in online networks. A community mindset looks beyond the "local" effect of such acts on the parties directly involved to consider the wider dynamics and implications that may follow in their wake. It is attentive to how audiences of friends and followers may feel about and respond to such incidents and how future actions may be informed, thus contributing to norms.

Almost one-quarter of the teens and young adults touched on the wider effects of negative online speech in their narratives about online life. One of the most explicit articulations of this mindset came from 15-year-old Trey, who spoke about his online postings as follows: "[I'm responsible to] anyone who uses Facebook and my profile or whatever. If I have something bad or offensive on there, it affects everyone."

More often, though, the "it's a community" mindset was more implicit in young people's narratives. For example, when describing the benefits and risks of online blogging, 20-year-old Christina reflected:

[Blogging is] a great way for people to vent their frustrations safely without hurting themselves or hurting others, like get their emotions out there, out of their head. Like, it's just easier for some people to blog and clear their heads and just calm down that way. But it's also a bad thing, definitely, especially if you leave it public. And if you're writing something kind of really mean and hurtful and someone else reads it, then that could hurt them and then rumors start, and then people start hating people for no good reason, like a bad snowball effect starts happening.

While not explicitly invoking the term, Christina alludes to community effects when she points to the "snowball effect" that "hurtful" speech can have when posted publicly.

Similarly, Maeve, age 11, shared her dismay about the negative tone she observes on Facebook: "People need to realize that these Web sites are not for—they're not for you to go online and get out all your anger. They're for you to go online and just have fun. Like Facebook wasn't made so that people could be fighting and be rude in their status. It was made so that people could interact with each other and show other people pictures, and stuff like that. But ... there shouldn't be any fighting."

Both Christina and Maeve described how online venues are often seized for expression of negative emotions—a function that runs counter to Maeve's understanding of the larger, prosocial purposes of social networks.

References to troubling speech acts—including mean comments and even bullying—were fairly prevalent among the tweens in our study. However, Maeve was the rare exception in alluding to the ethical or community effects of such speech. Most often, the tweens responded to such acts with narrower concerns—about consequences for perpetrators or with moral sensitivity (e.g., empathy) for the individual target. This is not surprising, given that capacities for more abstract, ethical considerations tend to be in development during the tween years.

That said, we did observe hints of ethical sensitivity among the tweens when prompted with a hypothetical scenario involving hate speech toward an unspecified race or religion. Just over half of the tweens perceived such speech as more troubling or "worse" than speech targeting an individual because it directly implicates a wide group of people.[40]

Overall, among the youths who engaged the "it's a community" mindset, troubling speech was one of the most frequently cited topics. We saw further evidence of this mindset among more than one-third of the teens and young adults who expressed concern that social cohesion was declining as a result of mediated communication in general and associated negative speech trends. Although none of the tweens made such pointed remarks about social cohesion, a few spoke to a related concern: that reliance on digital means of communication both multiplies and magnifies social conflicts among their friends and peers, thereby hinting at norms.

Community thinking is arguably an essential practice in the digital age. Given the reality that we post our thoughts, comments, photos, and other content in "networked publics" or in semipublic contexts, attention to the larger, community implications is critical.[41] Yet despite the impressive examples noted above, the "it's a community" mindset did not come up all that often, especially compared to other mindsets.

This is not to say that the young people with whom we spoke are not attuned to the effects of online content on others. Rather, as the "play nice" mindset revealed, the concerns they shared are typically narrower—keyed to the feelings, reactions, and experiences of a circumscribed group of participants whom they typically know offline. Yet even the empathetic stance represented by the "play nice" mindset was not invoked consistently, and some youths invoked it only rarely. For these young people, another mindset competes, and sometimes even supplants, the belief that online interactions should be guided by kindness and respect.

"It's Just the Internet"

Echoing the "it's just a game" mindset that we saw in the multiplayer game scenario, a number of youths expressed the mantra that "it's just the Internet"; in other words, what happens online has little value or significance. Just under one-third of the tweens and just over half of the teens and young adults with whom we spoke shared this attitude at some point in their interviews. Typical comments included language like the Internet "isn't real" and that what happens online "doesn't matter," so one "shouldn't take it to heart."

Peter, a college student and a musician, captured the "it's just the Internet" mindset well—even using those very words—when he described the dynamics among participants on a music blog he follows:

When someone talks trash, whether it's serious or not, you have to reply with ab-
surdity. Because ... you can't trust anything [so] you've got to be someone you can't
trust either. If you don't get that *it's just the Internet*—who cares ... especially on a
comment on a message board or some kind of board, it really doesn't matter. There's
no face to it, you're not actually saying anything to someone. So, even if it's a good
comment, it doesn't have as much weight as if you were standing in front of the
person and telling them. So it's even more true for talking shit. It's like if you go on
anonymously and call someone out on something, it's really cowardly, but you kind
of do [it]. So to counteract that, you just kind of make the whole thing a joke.

It is interesting that Peter trivializes both "talk[ing] trash" and "a good comment" being posted online; to him, the medium *is* the message: if it's conveyed online, you can't take it seriously.[42] In turn, after stating that "it's just
the Internet," Peter references a related belief: "the whole thing [is just] a
joke."

From youths of all ages, we frequently heard the attitude that much
of online speech—regardless of the cruelty suggested on the surface—was
arguably just a joke and should therefore be treated as such: either enjoyed
or disregarded. When we asked a subsample of teens and young adults about
different forms of self-expression online, nearly two-thirds dismissed "out-
going, gregarious," and "harmful or offensive conduct" as "just a joke."[43]

Internet norms suggesting that most online content is just for fun and
can be trivialized were often referenced as a basis for this mindset. When
we asked tweens about a hypothetical online hate group targeting a teacher,
nearly one-third either defended or made light of such speech. Just under
half of the youths dismissed the hate group as "funny" or "just a joke," and
another three tweens indicated that they might join in, depending on their
feelings about the teacher.[44]

Caleb, age 10, said, "It's not that bad. It's bad, but it's not serious. They
[are] just like joking with each other." Caleb imagined joking intentions
on the part of the youths, which allowed him to downplay their speech.
Brianna, age 14, read the situation somewhat differently: "I think it would
be funny. Like they're just being honest about what they think, and stuff
like that." In lauding the "honest" nature of the feelings being expressed,
Brianna alluded to free speech rights.

Both the "just a joke" mindset and the concern for free expression contribute here to tolerance of cruelty and sometimes even racism. Related
to this, in the Pew 2011 survey referred to earlier, 91 percent of the teens
reported that they most often ignore cruel behavior when they see it

online.[45] And in the Associated Press–MTV poll, 71 percent of the teens and young adults reported that people are more likely to use racist or sexist slurs via digital means than in person, and many of these youths dismissed the slurs as "just kidding."[46]

As part of the "it's just the Internet" mindset, we find the belief, exemplified by Caleb and Brianna, that the Internet is a free-flowing space to share one's thoughts, ideas, and whatever content is sure to amuse one's friends. This "anything goes" attitude is reflected in the often unreflective, and sometimes shocking, things youth share online. Photos of young people's partying activities, featuring alcohol use, are routinely shared on social networks despite the awareness of potential negative consequences.

Then there are cases in which more sensitive and damaging content has been shared, almost reflexively. In April 2010, a medical student at the State University of New York at Stonybrook was discovered to have posted a picture of a fellow student with a cadaver on Facebook in order to amuse her online friends. In the fallout, the student apologized for her "unquestionably egregious, idiotic, disrespectful, and thoughtless" decision to snap the photo and "exponentially worse, to have posted it on Facebook."[47]

The *Journal of the American Medical Association* published a survey indicating that similar incidents have occurred at medical schools across the United States, prompting efforts on some campuses to update ethics codes to reflect the realities of a networked world.[48] This development mirrors a broader trend in the professions and in the corporate world to hold employees to social media policies—even as some aspects of these policies are being challenged on free speech grounds.[49]

Finally, there have been a rash of disturbing cases in which images and even videos of sexual assaults have been posted on Twitter, Instagram, and other sites.[50] These egregious and "thoughtless" cases suggest significant blind spots regarding the effects of one's online content.

Mirroring the arguments explored in previous chapters that both privacy and property are forsaken on the Internet, the mindset that "it's just the Internet" can be dispiriting, especially for youths who feel more obligated than inspired to engage in social networks. Among some youths, we observed a sense of fatalism about the often insensitive, if not outright harmful, character of some online spaces.

Recall Peter's reflections about his participation in a less-than-civil blogging community: "You can't trust anything [so] you've got to be someone you can't trust either." Peter tailors his conduct and his online identity to suit the tone he observes. Nineteen-year-old John, a longtime participant in various online forums, shared:

> Most of the time when people see something online, their main reaction is to laugh because most of the stuff on the Internet you have no sway over at all, so you just laugh and move on. Then maybe show it to your friends at a party if you want to make them uncomfortable.... You're laughing. It's not the same psychological phenomenon, but [it's similar to] the Kitty Genovese [story].... I think in the 1930s [sic] or so, a woman was being killed ... in an alleyway. She screamed. Something like 50 [sic] people heard her, but none of them even dialed 911.
>
> It's kind of the same [on the Internet]. It's the same atmosphere, but I don't believe that it's the same psychological phenomenon.... Because with the Kitty Genovese thing, it's the fact that if there are 10 people in the room, each of them feels 10 percent responsible. But whereas on the Internet ... each person feels .001 percent responsible.... Each person is like, "I'm on the Internet, there's really nothing I can do. I know nothing about this person, so I'm just going to stand back and be a casual observer." And the Internet does turn a lot of interaction into casual observation or, at best, interested but still removed.[51]

John argued that the distance that is an indisputable feature of online interactions sharply reduces one's responsibility and efficacy in troubling interactions. As he put it, "most of the stuff on the Internet you have no sway over at all" and one is "at best, interested but still removed." So the default stance is to "just laugh and move on."

Related to this is a broader finding from our study: when we asked the teens and young adults about the sense of responsibility they felt online, very few youths spoke about a sense of responsibility beyond themselves and their closest offline relations. For many youths, hostile speech is perceived to be an entrenched element of Internet culture and thus often accepted, even if begrudgingly.

All told youth exhibit multiple and sometimes conflicting mindsets about conduct on the Internet. The "it's just the Internet" attitude is quite directly at odds with the "play nice" and "it's a community" mindsets. This dismissive mindset represents a conscious disconnect—as John's comments revealed—between individuals' online actions and the moral and ethical implications of those actions.

The narrow sense of responsibility many young people reported in relation to the Internet reflects an ethical blind spot: a failure to consider how their own participation, as well as their responses (or lack thereof) to the acts of others, inform the norms, integrity, and character of larger communities on the Web. Promoting greater attention to the ethical, community dimensions of conduct such as speech requires a concerted effort to understand the factors that underlie the stark disconnects and blind spots embedded in the "it's just the Internet" stance.

Accounting for Participation Blind Spots and Disconnects

As with privacy and property, a complex set of factors informs the mindsets that youth adopt regarding participation on the Internet. First, it is notable that the youths' narratives about troubling participation often implicated, and sometimes appeared to blame, the technological qualities and features of digital life. Youths of all ages spoke about qualities such as the distance between people online, the associated ease of sharing cruel content, the interpretive gap created by the lack of tone, and the permanence of online content.

As 14-year-old Max put it, "Online, everything's so definite.... Once something's said, it's said. In person, you can usually get your way out of it, if you didn't really mean it that way or whatever. But online if you say something and it really harms someone or offends someone, it's already there. It's on the record."

Opportunities for anonymity were also cited, especially by teens and young adults, such as Perry, age 17, "The anonymity of the Internet allows people to do stuff they wouldn't typically do, because they think they can get away with it or they can just be total jackasses and rude to everyone." Perry attributes the flaming, trolling, and other negative modes of speech he frequently observes to the opportunities for anonymity and the associated "disinhibition effect."[52]

Like Max and Perry, many youths strongly suggest that digital qualities contribute to problematic conduct. Yet the qualities by themselves are ethically neutral. More central is the way in which anonymity and the like are seized and managed, leading to good or ill. Awareness of the interpretive gap and other challenging qualities of the Web can certainly lead youth to be more thoughtful about the things they post. We saw some evidence of this in the "play nice" and "it's a community" mindsets.

However, the attitude that online content should be trivialized, dismissed, or treated like a joke also surfaced and, for some youths, dominates their approaches to the Internet. More central than digital affordances, then, are the individual, social, and cultural factors that feed these different mindsets.

Developmental factors may play a role in the extent to which tweens engage in different mindsets. The capacity for empathy, which is an aspect of moral thinking and the "play nice" mindset, is typically well developed by late childhood. However, the capacity to grasp the more distant implications of online speech and other acts for a larger community or public may still be in the process of development. Teens and young adults should be adept at both kinds of considerations. Yet their sensitivity to opportunities to engage in moral and ethical thinking, and their inclination to do so, is influenced by other factors.

An individual young person's beliefs, moral values, and extent of caring about others and the wider world should, in theory, influence the mindsets he or she adopts toward his or her own participation and that of others online. A number of young people invoked general moral principles, such as the Golden Rule, as guides for their choices both online and offline. However, others evinced a disconnect between the values they live by offline and their attitudes online. The dismissive "it's just the Internet" view reflects this disjuncture, and so does the broader finding that youths feel a narrower sense of responsibility online.

A factor that appears to mediate the extent to which a young person feels responsible to an online community is the degree to which he or she is invested, emotionally and otherwise, in its core activities. Thus, many committed bloggers, content creators, and gamers among our older youths displayed a clear sense of responsibility to their primary online activity. The community mindset appeared more often among these youths, and the "it's just the Internet" stance was rare. The youths who were more half-heartedly involved in ephemeral online communities, especially large online forums with frequently shifting discussion topics and membership, often articulated the "it's just the Internet" stance.

As we already noted, youth feel both compelled and excited to participate in social media because of its centrality as a space of peer sociality. Hence, their mindsets in these contexts are powerfully influenced not just by their own values but also by the rules and norms set by friends, followers, and the people they follow on Instagram, Tumblr, and Twitter. The moral and ethical climate of these networks can certainly be shaped by the presence or absence of formal community guidelines.[53]

Arguably more powerful, though, is the extent of "buy in" to such rules, which is displayed more informally. Teens and young adults in particular explicitly told us that the individuals who most influenced their online decision making were their peers. Friends' photos, "likes," retweets, and comments are where youth can detect social support for the "play nice," "it's a community," or "it's just the Internet" mindsets. Even when young people told us that they and their closest friends always "play nice" online, they almost always mentioned that offensive postings appeared, sometimes routinely, in their broader networks of online friends.

Some youths suggested that their default stance was to perceive most online content as just a joke and ignore it. By-standing was also documented by Pew's 2011 survey, in which 95 percent of teens reported that they've seen their peers ignore online cruelty.[54] Inaction is somewhat understandable, given the potential for peer backlash, online or offline, that may follow upstanding acts on public or semipublic social media sites.

Broader cultural influences also affect the mindsets young people assume vis-à-vis online participation. The belief in the Web as a site of free expression has broad support. Among the most widely touted promises of the Internet is the democratization of speech. Yet this promise has its drawbacks as hate speech and other troubling content proliferate online. Among the most critical dilemmas of the digital age is how to respond to hate speech while preserving the openness of the Web. Some social media sites (such as Facebook) crack down on explicitly hateful speech, whereas others (such as Twitter) are staunch protectors of such speech as a First Amendment right.[55]

Some thinkers argue that unrestrained speech is for the good because hate can be addressed only when it's visible. Others argue that some speech should be curbed in the interest of creating a more respectful and inviting Web; for example, threatening misogynist speech has been shown to silence some female bloggers.[56] Either way, participants who post harmful content are, in effect, unwitting role models, or antimentors, for young people. And they are often adults.

In the fall of 2012, a controversy emerged on Reddit, a social news community that engages more than 19 million participants a month. The site is made up of user-generated discussion threads called *sub-reddits* on pretty much any topic you can imagine—and some that you can't. The trouble started when users began to complain about a sub-reddit called Creepshots whose main purpose was to share, ogle, and comment on pictures of young women and underage girls taken and uploaded without their knowledge and consent.

Adrian Chen, a journalist at a Web site called Gawker, wrote an article in which he publicly outed, or "doxxed," Creepshots's creator, a 49-year-old computer programmer who went by the pseudonym Violentacrez, revealing his real identity. Dubbing him "the biggest troll on the Web," Chen revealed how Violentacrez had, over several years, created offensive sub-reddits with names such as RapeBait, Hitler, and Misogyny.[57]

The Gawker piece led to significant offline consequences for Violentacrez, who was fired from his job and lost his health insurance—the latter a significant consequence for his family, since his wife is disabled. A volatile discussion ensued in the Reddit community. A number of prominent Reddit users rallied to Violentacrez's defense, and they also defended their own right to act anonymously in setting up sub-reddits as they wished, regardless of the content. Yet others pushed back on the notion that free speech and privacy should be protected for Violentacrez yet not for the women whose photographs were shared without their consent. Ultimately the Creepshots sub-reddit was deleted, but similar sub-reddits continue to pop up on the site on a routine basis, according to Chen.

Perhaps even more unsettling are the cases in which so-called public servants engage in public hate speech on social media sites, and with their real names attached. In chapter 1, I described the 2011 revelation of a public Facebook group launched by a group of New York City police officers to complain about the annual West Indian Day Parade. The page included racist, nonanonymous comments referring to parade participants as "savages" and "animals."[58]

These two cases are notable examples of adults tapping the free speech environment of the Web in ways that suggest dramatic blind spots regarding the rights and integrity of others. Moreover, these figures are mentors— or rather, antimentors—who set examples for young Reddit and Facebook participants. Although these are fairly dramatic cases of antimentoring, you don't have to look too deeply on the Web to find further examples. As I have noted, disrespect is arguably normative in the comments sections of news sites.

Although we cannot draw a direct causal connection from online speech and the arguments in its defense to the mindsets youth adopt, neither can we ignore that this is part of the larger ecology of the Internet that youth experience. Moreover, teens and young adults explicitly told us that norma-tive conduct on specific online communities influenced their approaches to the Web.

Youths can react in various ways to this cultural backdrop. They may commit to be conscientious in their own postings and in their comments about others' content, they may join in the hateful banter, or they may avoid confronting others' negative speech when they see it. There are understandable risks associated with public upstanding in the face of cruel speech on social media sites, yet inaction has its costs, too.[59]

A few young people in our study stated explicitly that they tolerated, and looked away from, troubling speech not because they took it as a joke but on free speech grounds. Jeffrey, age 25, shared, "I've seen people put down things like very racist stuff.... I'm tempted to flag it, you know, but I don't ... because I believe in free speech. The First Amendment is really valuable. And I may not agree with—I obviously don't agree with it, but that person, I believe, has the right to express that "Heil Hitler" or what-ever, even though I abhor it, because it's a slippery slope."

Jeffrey's commitment to free speech is in obvious tension with his desire to confront racist speech when he sees it. Even though he is offended by some of the comments his "friends'" posts, his belief in unfettered free speech contributes to a by-standing disposition rather than an inclination to use his own right of speech to confront them.

One can certainly avoid offensive speech altogether by "unfollowing" or "unfriending" people, hiding their status updates, and avoiding online forums, networks, and sites known for volatile exchanges. However, such choices contribute to the problem of exposure to only like-minded people and points of view, thus undermining cosmopolitanism, a key promise of the Web.[60]

The Word from Adults: What Youth Hear about Online Participation

When we examine the role of proximate adults—parents, teachers, and other offline figures in youth's lives—we confront a mixed picture of their involvement and influence. The older youths in our studies reported rela-tively few conversations with adults about conduct on the Internet. Less than 15 percent of these youths said that a close adult figure—such as a parent, an aunt, an uncle, or a teacher—had an influence on their online choices. However, through school assemblies and public service announcements, they heard occasional messages about cyberbullying, "stranger danger," and the risks of sharing inappropriate content (i.e., content that could get them into trouble).

Parents have a much stronger presence in the online lives of tweens, offering advice and often directly monitoring their social networking lives in particular. The frequency of the messages these youths hear about the Internet probably explains the fact that fewer of them evinced the "it's just the Internet" stance than teens and young adults.

According to the tweens, the most frequent messages they hear are warnings against posting content that could get them into trouble or put them at risk of "stranger danger." Some youths learn about such risks at school, too. School-based cyberbullying conversations were mentioned by just under half of the tweens. Some tweens told us that they valued the advice of their parents and other adults about the Internet. Yet less than one-quarter of the tweens told us they would actively turn to an adult if they witnessed cruel speech toward an individual or group online.[61] Again, the belief that such speech is often just a joke was cited here, along with the related argument that adults would misinterpret and escalate the situation unnecessarily.

Adults too evinced a mix of mindsets in their own approaches to the Internet. The "play nice" and "it's a community" stances toward online content appeared, to various degrees, among adults. It is notable that none of the parents and teachers held the mindset of "it's just the Internet." Yet, as with privacy and property, consequence-oriented concerns were also prevalent in relation to online speech.

When we presented parents and teachers with a hypothetical scenario involving negative online speech about one's employer, the overwhelming majority gave responses that were, above all, attentive to the likelihood of the perpetrator getting into trouble or fired from his or her job. Although moral and ethical concerns came up occasionally, consequences loomed larger. These adults, like the youths we observed, showed greater moral and ethical sensitivity to a scenario related to hate speech about a racial or religious group. Yet here too we heard nearly one-quarter approaching the scenario with strictly consequence-oriented concerns.

When talking about how their own children and students manage their online lives, the adults often paid more significant attention to personal safety or possible risks to the youths' futures from posting inappropriate content on Facebook and other sites. These data stand as further evidence of a mentorship gap in relation to moral and ethical dilemmas on the Internet.

Conclusion

In this chapter, I have explored egregious forms of participation on the Web that illuminate often deep tensions between individual expression and the larger community. This is not to suggest that there aren't places on the Web where the individual and the community are aligned; the promises of the Internet are certainly being realized in some online communities.[62] Still, we should not turn a blind eye to the counterexamples. Efforts to "game the Internet" to one's personal advantage are all too frequent. Moreover, overtly racist, misogynist, antigay, and other forms of hate speech are also pervasive to an unfortunate degree on the Web, perpetrated by anonymous and identifiable participants alike.

I began with a dilemma about cheating new players in the MMOG context. I then shifted my attention to nongame online forums—such as Facebook, Twitter, or Reddit—where "it's just a game" or "it's not real" attitudes can hardly hold up. I considered young people's stances toward negative speech in these contexts and found three distinct mindsets, including an "it's just the Internet" stance that trivializes most content on the Web.

This mindset thwarts and almost mocks morally and ethically concerned approaches marked by empathy and the integrity of online communities. It serves as another example of both a blind spot and sometimes a mindful disconnect—in this case, between online speech acts and their effects on their targets and on the climate of the sites on which such acts unfold. Indeed, this mindset seizes on the myth that the distance and anonymity that mark the Web mean that we are disconnected from one another when in fact we are deeply, irrevocably interconnected, part of something larger than ourselves. Notably, youth who are deeply invested in and authentically connected to online communities are less likely to exhibit disconnects and blind spots about the moral and ethical dimensions of participation.

The troubling cases explored in this chapter suggest the need for a broader and deeper sense of responsibility for the "digital afterlives" of our own actions, for the actions of others we observe, and for the moral and ethical status of the communities we take part in constructing online. In the next chapter, I put forth an argument for conscientious connectivity and consider the various fronts through which it may be cultivated.

5   Correcting the Blind Spots, Reconnecting the Disconnects

One Last Dramatic Case

In August 2012, a heavily intoxicated teenage girl was sexually assaulted by high school football players after passing out at a party in Steubenville, Ohio. For several hours, she was dragged around, taken from party to party, and subjected to multiple acts of sexual violence. Several bystanders took photos and videos with their cell phones and shared them with others via Instagram, Facebook, Twitter, and text-messaging. One tweet read, "Song of the night is definitely Rape Me by Nirvana." A 12½-minute video in which onlookers joked about the assaults was posted on YouTube. Although the parents, teachers, and coaches of the youths involved tried to trivialize the incident, it became difficult to do so in the face of these digital artifacts. Some digital content became key evidence in the criminal proceedings against the perpetrators.[1]

The Steubenville rape case stands as a dramatic example of the human capacity for brutality and callousness. It also sheds light on the ways in which digital media can be used to magnify evil. Rape—a horrific crime on its own—is magnified when depictions of it are spread via social media. The victim's suffering is extended as the indignities she experienced are made accessible to a wide public. Moreover, the tweets, photos, and video suggest to others—especially other men—that such treatment of women is appropriate, even worthy of bragging about.

Yet the digital artifacts from this incident also serve as indisputable evidence of—and may help us understand—the attitudes and social dynamics that contribute to rape, to by-standing behavior, and to a larger rape culture. As sociologist Sarah Sobieraj argues, the social media evidence in this case provides "a rare window into rape. What we find makes the cultural myths that serve to silence victims and excuse perpetrators far more difficult to maintain. Watching the video and seeing the laughter, hearing the braggadocio, it becomes harder to assert that those football players are 'nice kids,' and nearly impossible to sustain the idea that the event was an unfortunate 'miscommunication,' or that this was 'just a stupid mistake.'"[2]

Throughout this book, I have described other dramatic cases: privacy invasion via webcam, posting of young women's photos without their knowledge or consent, the overreaching appropriation of others' creative work, and the use of the Internet to voice racist and inhumane speech. These acts reveal how digital media can be used in deeply troubling ways that harm, and sometimes utterly devastate, other people. As Sobieraj suggests in relation to the Steubenville case, however, the Internet doesn't simply magnify such harm; it also brings attention to it and can provide opportunities for discussing and addressing it. Yet the extent to which digital documentation of these incidents serve as wake-up calls where they matter most is unclear.

What Were They Thinking?

In all these dramatic cases, a crucial question surfaces: What were the perpetrators of these acts *thinking*? It's hard to say for sure. But it's pretty clear what they *weren't* thinking about: the bodily integrity of the young woman being assaulted, the right to privacy and the dignity of Tyler Clementi and of the young women whose photos were shared on Reddit, the feelings of the writer whose words were simply replicated without attribution, and the public nature of the Internet and the persistence of content there. In some instances, these thinking gaps represent true blind spots: the complete failure to recognize the moral and ethical dimensions of one's choices. In other instances, we perceive more mindful disconnects: the awareness of a moral or ethical situation but a decision to proceed with a harmful course of action nonetheless.

Despite these thinking lapses, most of these young people may be caring individuals with moral and ethical values. So what went awry? Why and how did their values fade into the background? How did digital technologies, and the social and culture norms around their use, contribute? What alternative beliefs, values, and agendas influenced their actions? Given the reality that digital media magnify the effects of our choices, both good and bad, sorting out these questions is urgent.

In this book, I have explored the ways of thinking and mindsets that young people bring to their mediated interactions with intimates and unknown individuals alike. In my analysis, I was not looking for evidence of right versus wrong approaches or courses of action. Rather, I sought to understand the extent to which youth perceive moral and ethical dilemmas and seek to grapple with them. My exploration *did* uncover inspiring, morally and ethically sensitive approaches to online life among the tweens, teens, and young adults in our study.

However, these bright spots exist alongside troubling blind spots, mindful disconnects, and deeply individualistic approaches to the Internet. In attending to the deficits, my narrative is more of a "glass half empty" portrait of the digital world. Indeed, my purpose in writing this book is to call attention to the more troubling dispositions in online life and to explore their subtleties and their links to broader mindsets, cultural ideologies, and social supports—including messages from adults.

Although I have framed the issues with extreme cases, I have also attended to the less dramatic but potentially problematic dimensions of routine, everyday online practices and decisions: posting pictures of friends at a bar, commenting on a friend's new profile picture, "liking" an online group whose purpose is to complain about a teacher, getting and sharing music and other fun content found on the Web, and scamming new players in MMOGs.

Regardless of our intentions, the online content we post, "like," or retweet can be misread, taken out of context, copied, forwarded, and otherwise misused in ways that harm our friends, family members, peers, colleagues, and online connections. We can readily appropriate other people's content, whether or not they invite us to. We can also manipulate the inherent distance between ourselves and others online and take advantage of the opportunities to be anonymous to cheat, to disrespect, and even to bully others. Therefore, what we do online has moral significance.

Moreover, situated as they are in public networks, our online choices have the potential to touch countless lives; therefore, our actions have ethical significance, too. The choices we make about others' content and the ways we treat one another in general can affect other people—those we can't see and may never know personally. Our actions, and our inaction in the face of harm, also help to set or solidify social norms.

The Good Stuff

The moral significance of online privacy, property, and participation was recognized by many of the youths we interviewed. In fact, they were quite adept at engaging empathy and other aspects of moral thinking vis-à-vis online commenting, photo posting, and other everyday digital acts. In relation to online privacy, we observed that many youths had a "privacy as social" mindset and that some asserted a moral responsibility to be mindful of other people's privacy in digital contexts. Shades of the "play nice" mindset featured in the participation chapter were invoked here, especially when the youths spoke about how they avoided sharing potentially embarrassing content or information about friends online.

Sensitivity to the broader ethical dimensions of online sharing decisions was less prevalent, but a few young people were mindful that the content they chose to share online set an example for a larger community.

In relation to property, we found that some youths took seriously the importance of respecting other people's creative work—whether music, artwork, video, or words—and considering how the creators might be affected if their work was used without attribution or downloaded without payment. Some young people considered how the illicit appropriation of others' content, as in music piracy, could have more distant, negative effects on the music industry.

A few others showed ethical sensitivity in relation to property issues by questioning the fairness and ethical status of the creative industries and of intellectual property restrictions. Youths in creator roles, such as blogging and content creation, were often more sensitive to the moral and ethical dimensions of these issues.

When the youths considered the ethics of participation on the Internet, many of them evinced a morally sensitive, "play nice" mindset that favored empathetic perspective taking, Golden Rule thinking, and being fair to people. The ethical connotations of online conduct were acknowledged by some youths in the form of an "it's a community" mindset. We noticed that young people who are deeply invested in particular online communities—such as those focused on an activity like blogging, content creation, or gaming—were more likely to invoke such ethically sensitive mindsets.

The Gap

Impressive as these conscientious mindsets are, they often exist in some youths alongside deeply individualistic, dismissive, and even downright callous mindsets. Individualistic ways of thinking, sharply focused on consequences for the self, dominated most young people's considerations when they confronted online privacy and property situations in particular. Self-centered stances are not surprising given that egocentrism often characterizes the adolescent and emerging adulthood phases of development. However, the dominance of egocentric thinking is problematic online, given the deeply social nature of the Internet and the qualities and opportunities that can link our seemingly parochial choices to distant people and a wide public.

There were also more overtly troubling mindsets that supported moral and ethical lapses. The "privacy as forsaken" mindset, while invoked by some youths as an argument for treating others' privacy with care, in other cases appeared to contribute to a lax attitude toward privacy lapses. Similarly, the free-for-all mindset that was engaged vis-à-vis online property issues can be rooted in a cogent ethical argument for the Internet as a "creative commons." However, most youths who adopted this stance had a more self-serving interpretation: "free for me."

The most explicitly troubling mindset surfaced in relation to online participation and was marked by the belief that anything that happens online can be trivialized; in other words, "It's just the internet." Related to this was the mantra that much of online speech is "just a joke." Mindsets that suggest that what we do online is insignificant, trivial, or just for laughs are out of step with the reality that what we share online has a "digital afterlife" that may be largely out of our hands.[3]

The youths in our study were often inconsistent in the mindsets they invoked in various online situations and contexts. A few young people were flagrantly inconsistent: paying deep attention to ethical concerns in relation to one theme, such as property, yet evincing a moral disconnect in relation to another, such as online privacy. However, the more typical pattern involved morally sensitive mindsets (concern for known others) yet blind spots regarding the ethical dimensions of online choices (concern for distant others and communities).

This finding is consistent with the argument that empathy, with its focus on a singular, often known, human face, is inspired more readily than concern for a larger systemic, community, or global issue, which requires a more abstract disposition.[4] At the same time, as I've argued in numerous places in this book, living in a digitally, globally interconnected world elevates the importance of ethical thinking.

Our research therefore points to the existence of an ethics gap. Although most youth have the capacity for ethical thinking, this capacity isn't consistently tapped. Individualistic approaches to the Internet are widespread, ethical blind spots are commonplace, and disconnects appear with some regularity. This evidence of "bounded ethicality" coexists uneasily with the "boundlessness" of our actions in a digital age.[5]

Accounting for the Ethics Gap

How youth think about and navigate the digital world is influenced by a complex set of factors: their ethical capacities and dispositions, social pressures and norms, signals from other people's conduct, and explicit messages about do's and don'ts online.

There are undeniable developmental aspects of the ethics gap. Although humans develop the capacity to be morally sensitive in early childhood, the capacities for ethical thinking develop later, typically in early adolescence. Therefore, we can expect tweens to engage in empathetic perspective taking, but they are likely to need support to recognize the broader, more distant implications of their online actions. Teens and young adults, in contrast, typically have the capacity to think about how their actions fit into a broader community.

As I've noted throughout this book, however, capacity is not enough; indeed, it may be the least challenging piece of the puzzle. Sensitivity to the moral or ethical dimensions of a situation is the more frequent stumbling block.[6] Youths first need to recognize when sharing a photo or another piece of content online might constitute a moral or an ethical dilemma, not simply a personal one. Furthermore, once sensitized to the moral or ethical dimensions of a scenario, they need to be motivated to wrestle with the associated dilemmas.

There are social and cultural dimensions to the ethics gap, too. Engaged in critical stages of identity formation and exploration, young people are often both more self-absorbed and subject to the influence of social, peer-driven concerns.[7] The conduct of friends and peers in online social networks, blogs, and games can exert a powerful influence on young people's sense of what is "fair game" online. Sharing embarrassing photos of peers and posting, forwarding, or ignoring hurtful comments may be normative in youths' online circles. Fitting in may mean "liking," retweeting, or simply scrolling past the mean stuff.

Peers may not be the only contributor here. Adult antimentors can be found across the Web—bickering and bullying in the comments sections of news sites, engaging in racist speech on Facebook, posting illicit photos of teenage girls on Reddit. These incidental role models convey powerful and deeply troubling messages about what these online spaces can be used for.

The more purposeful mentors in young peoples' lives—parents, educators, and other nearby adults—are arguably poised to influence youth's moral and ethical dispositions vis-à-vis the Web. Yet our interviews with both youth and adults suggest a series of missed opportunities here. Adult conversations with youth typically focus on "stranger danger," protecting one's own privacy, and avoiding posting content that could get one kicked out of school or fired from a job. As we discussed in chapter 2, approaching online privacy as an individual responsibility in many ways misses the mark—privacy is no longer truly in our own hands. Failing to acknowledge the social and, indeed, moral elements of privacy in a digital age is a missed opportunity to encourage youth to develop more robust, social approaches toward online privacy that are built on respect.[8]

Similarly, adult conversations with youth about attribution and property issues do not appear to engage deeply with what it means to respect creative work. Nor do the typical discussions about property involve pointing out and grappling with the ethical dimensions of piracy, intellectual property law, and the profit structure of the creative industries. Regarding participation, although some youths reported conversations with adults about bullying in the strict sense of the term, more subtle acts of cruelty and social exclusion often experienced online did not appear to be brought up and addressed.[9]

Overall, adult conversations with youth often contribute to and strengthen the blind spots we often observed among youth. Thus, a key component of the ethics gap is the mentorship gap. Although parents and educators may be well-intentioned in their emphasis on personal safety, their overattention to such concerns leaves little room for discussions about ethics and social responsibility on the Web. This mentorship gap may also result in insufficient support for youth to successfully utilize the great promises of the Web, such as the opportunity to participate in civic and political life.[10]

A New Ethics Gap? (Or Just an Old One with a New Spin?)

A key question regarding the digital ethics gap is the extent to which it is new—born directly of the Internet and related digital developments— or has deeper, nondigital roots. Arguably, the drivers of moral and ethical development—and of moral and ethical lapses—for young people growing up digital may not be all that different from those experienced by youth who grew up in the predigital era. Yet we need to be mindful of how the qualities of online contexts and the related habits of connectivity interact with the psychological, social, and cultural dynamics of young people's, and adults', lives in ways that sometimes allow moral and ethical concerns to fade from view.

The qualities and affordances of online life undoubtedly create new moral and ethical challenges. Communicating with others from behind a screen may not feel as real as face-to-face encounters do. If we choose to communicate anonymously, we may feel even more removed from others and perhaps disinhibited in ways that contribute to positive as well as negative exchanges. The distance between our actions and their actual effects on other people may be invisible to us or difficult to grasp.[11]

Related to this is the gap between the intended meaning behind the things we post and the ways in which they are received by others. Moreover, the reality that what we say online persists, can be copied and searched for, and is scalable raises the stakes around our communications.[12] Perhaps more essential are the habits of connectivity that we, and especially young people, have developed. Being "always on," constantly connected, and often in a multitasking mode creates little space to reflect on what we post and observe, to spot potentially troubling implications, and to grapple with any related dilemmas.[13]

Furthermore, perhaps the new conditions of life wrought by the Internet and digital technologies require wholly new ethical frameworks. This question has been the subject of debate among philosophers and other thinkers. Philosopher Herman Tavani explores this issue directly and persuasively concludes that, at the current historical moment at least, "our core moral notions—that is, agency, autonomy, respect for persons, responsibility, and so on" endure despite new complexities posed by the digital age.[14] However, he also notes that the moral and ethical dimensions of digital technologies such as search engines are not always immediately evident and thus require careful consideration, dialogue, and perhaps new policies regarding their use.

So even though new ethical frameworks might not be warranted, there may be cause for more reflective approaches. Luciano Floridi and J. W. Sanders argue that the digital era requires constructionist, proactive ethical approaches.[15] Therefore, minding the ethics gap means nurturing reflective, conscientious habits of mind to accompany our habits of connectivity. In other words, we need to cultivate conscientious connectivity.

Toward Conscientious Connectivity

I now turn to the puzzle of how we might narrow the ethics gap and cultivate more conscious, and conscientious, ways of "being digital."[16] My thinking about this problem area is informed by key ideas from behavioral ethics, moral education, thinking dispositions literature, and the work of our larger research group at Project Zero.

The concept of *conscientious connectivity* is my answer to the troubling blind spots and disconnected mindsets that have been the focus of my attention throughout this book. This concept has affinities with the popular psychological concept of "mindfulness." Worth noting here is Howard Rheingold's book, *Net Smart*, an argument for mindfulness as a key ingredient of "thriving online" amid a multitude of distractions. But conscientious connectivity is above all targeted to matters of the conscience. In this way, it resonates with psychologist Scott Reynolds's concept of "moral attentiveness," which involves a disposition to be proactively on the lookout for the moral or ethical dimensions of various situations.[17]

Conscientious connectivity is an ethical disposition toward the digital world; it engages the key components of a thinking disposition: skills, sensitivity, and inclination.[18] It is specifically marked by the use of ethical thinking skills, a sensitivity to the moral and ethical dimensions of online situations, and a motivation to reflect on and wrestle with the associated dilemmas. It also implies action, which requires a sense of agency in relation to the integrity of the Web. I will now consider each element of conscientious connectivity in turn, with examples of what it can look like in practice.

Engaging Ethical Thinking Skills

I begin with describing ethical thinking skills, in part because they are implicated in the other dimensions of conscientious connectivity, especially sensitivity but also motivation and agency. In chapter 1, I referred to three ethical thinking skills that informed our research team's analysis of youth's thinking: roles and responsibility thinking, complex perspective taking, and community thinking.[19] These skills are also at the heart of the educational efforts of our Good Play Project and of our collaborators at Common Sense Media and Project New Media Literacies (described further in the "Educational Fronts" section below).

Complex perspective taking involves paying attention to multiple stakeholders who might be implicated in or affected by an online action such as posting a photo, downloading a piece of music, or contributing to Wikipedia.[20] Given that online spaces are public networks subject to the risk of "context collapse," the consideration of both known others and distant unknown others is an essential part of complex perspective taking.[21]

One example is considering how one's Instagram photos of a fun night at the bar might be seen, interpreted, and received by different audiences. Another is recognizing that sarcastic or ironic online comments may be received as intended by certain audiences but be read quite differently by others. In these ways, complex perspective taking is a way of minding the interpretive gap that often accompanies online speech acts.

Roles and responsibilities thinking involves attention to one's offline and online roles: student at a particular school, daughter or son, member of a soccer league, employee of an organization, community leader, Wikipedian, creator of a Facebook social cause group, or guild leader in *World of Warcraft*. Consideration of the implied responsibilities associated with the myriad roles one assumes—and especially the individuals and communities to whom one is responsible—is central to this type of thinking.[22]

Roles and responsibilities thinking might involve considering how a sarcastic or disrespectful tweet about one's employer or principal could reflect back on the company one works for or the school one attends—especially if affiliation to the company or school is indicated in one's profile. Use of the sentence "Tweets are my own" in a profile is one way in which some Twitter users have sought to manage this issue. Although this gesture may be imperfect, it does represent an acknowledgment of the roles and responsibilities quandary on the Web.

Community thinking is attentive to the potential benefit and harm an online action could have to a larger community, society, or world. This thinking move might involve considering how a YouTube video depicting a fight between classmates may influence the integrity and climate of YouTube and implicitly encourage violence as an appropriate mode of conflict resolution at school. Similarly, a gamer might consider how the larger economy of an MMOG might be influenced by a decision to cheat.

The trio of ethical skills described here may not be exhaustive, but when they are engaged they can help direct one's thinking to key moral and ethical considerations with which to grapple. Yet confronting the ethics gap requires more than ethical thinking skills; it also requires a disposition to tune in to the dilemmas and to care.

Cultivating Ethical Sensitivity (Correcting the Blind Spots)

Blind spots—failures to be sensitive to moral or ethical issues when they arise—are a significant piece of the ethics gap. Correcting blind spots necessarily involves cultivating ethical sensitivity. Here, the focus is on acknowledging possible moral and ethical issues, perceiving the dilemmas, and recognizing the stakes that may be at play.

Experts in behavioral ethics suggest various strategies for confronting blind spots that are adaptable to online situations.[23] For example, deliberating about real or hypothetical online scenarios—and analyzing various ways of thinking about them, including the likelihood of defaulting to simplistic, self-focused considerations—is one way of cognitively priming oneself to recognize ethical issues when they come up.

Throughout this book, I have described both dramatic and everyday dilemmas and posed related questions with the aim of triggering your sensitivity to areas of moral and ethical concern. Similarly, we designed the scenarios used in our studies to explore the extent to which youth were sensitive to these issues. In chapter 2, I opened with the tagged scenario in which a Facebook photo revealed that a young person had breached a team policy, attending a party the night before a big playoff game. Although most youths to whom we presented this scenario offered a knee-jerk "untag me" response, upon further probing and reflection, some youths at least recognized broader considerations.

Scenarios such as these can be seen not only as research tools but also as ethics-spotting exercises.[24] They can be particularly successful when combined with short thinking routines: questions that reveal one's think-ing and make it visible, as a first step toward deeper reflection.[25] Encourag-ing awareness of the nature and targets of one's thinking (e.g., self, known others, or a larger community) can prompt reflection about one's "universe of obligation" or responsibility.[26] Engaging in perspective-taking exercises— taking a "circle of viewpoints"—can also expose moral and ethical points of view and stakes that might otherwise go unrecognized.[27] In relation to the tagged scenario, this would involve considering the effects of one's actions on different stakeholders: the coach, the teammates, other students on campus, the larger school community, and more distant audiences for online photos.

Ethics-spotting exercises such as these can be powerful mechanisms for engendering ethical sensitivity. Yet perceiving the issues at stake is only the first step. As psychologist Richard Weissbourd suggests, perspective tak-ing is not enough; you have to value the perspectives you take.[28] The next step is to cultivate the motivation to care about and truly wrestle with the dilemmas.

Cultivating Motivation (Reconnecting the Disconnects)

Reconnecting the disconnects—the inclination of some online participants to dismiss or trivialize the moral and ethical implications of their choices— is arguably the most challenging puzzle. The problem here is not sensitivity, attentiveness, or mindfulness; rather, it is moral and ethical *motivation*—the inclination to wrestle deeply with the dilemmas and perspectives at hand. Motivation hinges on the extent to which one *cares* about someone tagged in or on the receiving end of one's status update, Tweet, or blog post.

Given our often unreflective habits of connectivity, exercises and rou-tines that remind and even provoke us to consider our deeply held values and sense of caring for others are warranted. Providing youth with frequent opportunities to name and reflect on their moral beliefs and values is one way of encouraging them to access their sense of caring. My colleagues at the Good Project have devised powerful but lean structures for incit-ing these kinds of reflections. For example, the Good Project value-sort exercise involves arranging a set of values—such as honesty, caring, and independence—into a hierarchy based on one's priorities.[29] The mirror test involves metaphorically (or even literally) looking in a mirror and consid-ering whether one's actions align with one's cherished values. Carried out habitually, this reflective routine may engender greater moral and ethical motivation.

The extent to which young people, and all of us, are disposed to engage with moral and ethical concerns is ultimately an identity issue. If concern for others, both near and far, is not a priority, then blind spots and disconnects are to be expected. A complex set of factors is at play here for young people; educators, parents, siblings, and peers are all pivotal influences, and so are messages and support from the wider culture. On a practical level, thoughtful, ethically sensitive identities can be cultivated when dialogue about moral and ethical issues is a regular part of a young person's life—when frequent support and incentives exist for grappling with and debating dilemmas in light of different moral beliefs, values, and interests. Although the suggestions I've raised here are not magic solutions, they are arguably worthwhile steps in the right direction.

The suggested strategies for engaging ethical skills, sensitivity, and motivation overlap in various ways. They also require time and focused attention—precious commodities in our connected lives.[30] Yet the dilemmas that are explored in this book surface when we are online—when our attention may be divided among different tasks, while instant messages are asking for immediate responses, and as we are perpetually inundated with new stimuli. The cognitive and emotional work of reflecting on different perspectives, considering one's roles and responsibilities, and grappling deeply with dilemmas may therefore require routine digital time-outs.

Cultivating Agency

A final element of conscientious connectivity is agency: the capacity to envision and enact socially positive or civic online deeds. Digitally savvy youth have tremendous powers at their fingertips. Yet they may feel little efficacy in the face of online scenarios, especially the disrespect and outright cruelty that is arguably normative in some online spaces. Nevertheless, there are shining examples of youths, and adults, who use the Web to confront social concerns and to promote a greater good.

One college student we interviewed uses her video blog and YouTube channel to promote thoughtful conversations about important issues affecting her community. Her videos feature interviews with community members about issues such as domestic violence. She sees her online presence as a positive force for change offline *and* on the Web, where it stands as a counterexample to some of the negative exchanges she witnesses on social media sites.

Further examples of agency have surfaced in studies of the Internet and activism. As part of a new research network on youth and participatory politics, our team is studying how civically engaged youths leverage social media and other digital affordances for their causes. For example, one teen described her strategic use of Facebook to create dialogue and social action plans in response to the growing problem of youth violence in her community.

Certainly, such acts of "participatory politics" can go wrong in various ways: misinformation can be spread, complex issues can be oversimplified, and dialogue can devolve into shouting matches.[31] Online speech acts of a political nature can also be misinterpreted or incite negative backlash.[32] Ethical thinking skills, among other competencies, are therefore essential companions to these modes of action. Above all, though, these practices can inspire youth to envision alternative ways of being digital.

These four key elements of conscientious connectivity—ethical thinking skills, ethical sensitivity, motivation, and agency—can act as counterforces to blind spots, disconnects, and the tendency to withdraw from troubling exchanges observed on the Web. Now that I've sketched this vision and described its key ingredients, I turn to a consideration of potential entry points through which to cultivate conscientious habits of connectivity.

Entry Points

The key question here is this: Who is responsible for confronting the kinds of blind spots and disconnects that I have explored in these pages? Who is responsible for the ill-considered choices of the college student who used a webcam to invade his roommate's privacy, of the young writer who blithely appropriated the work of another person, of the medical student who posted a picture of herself with a cadaver on Facebook, of the Ohio teens who callously tweeted about the sexual assault of a girl as they witnessed it, and of the New York police officers who created and participated in a racist Facebook group about the citizens they were charged with protecting and serving?

Who is responsible for the larger population of digital youths making more routine, but still morally and ethically loaded, decisions about what to say, share, and do online? Below I explore possible answers to the responsibility question by considering various entry points, or fronts, for closing the ethics gap and cultivating conscientious connectivity.

Digital Fronts

Social media, search engine, and other technology companies are incredibly powerful today. The amount of data we give them—willingly, and often without reference to their "terms and conditions"—is stunning. On a fundamental level, technology companies influence our conduct through the affordances and constraints built into the technologies they develop. The design of apps, social media sites, games, and interactive Web sites lays the groundwork for how we engage with one another and with content. Computer scientist and writer Jaron Lanier argues that technology "locks in" certain possibilities and shuts off others.[33]

To what extent and how might technology be utilized to cultivate moral and ethical thinking? Social media sites could certainly build in features, such as pop-up windows that ask us questions ("Are you sure you want to make this photo public?") and remind us to reflect on our choices.

Digital designers could also build in features that invite or require us to attribute when we draw on others' content. For example, as discussed in chapter 3, the online computer programming community Scratch contains a feature that automatically attributes the original creator of a work when someone else remixes or builds on it. Nevertheless, a study of Scratch users showed that they preferred it when remixers went out of their way to acknowledge them rather than simply relying on the technology for attribution.[34]

Similarly, the use of the Turnitin antiplagiarism tool to check students' work for plagiarism, while helpful to teachers, does little to help students' proactively consider how and when they should draw on someone else's work.[35] Relying on technology to remind us to be ethical, or simply to catch us when we fail to be so, may actually work against the development of the moral and ethical thinking skills, sensitivity, and motivation required to confront life's complex ethical challenges, both online and offline.[36]

Social media and other technology companies can influence us in other ways as well. Sites such as Facebook and, more recently, *Huffington Post*, require participants to use their real names in an effort to encourage civility.[37] The guidelines that sites set and the decisions they make about how to respond to hateful speech, cheating, privacy lapses, and appropriation of content function as ground rules for participation. Internet legal scholar Jeffrey Rosen recently argued that Facebook, Google, and Twitter "have more power over who can speak and what can be said all across the globe than any king or president or Supreme Court justice."[38]

Nevertheless, there is some evidence to suggest that site guidelines have a limited effect, because some participants on social media sites routinely flout them. Sanctions or removal from a site can be a more powerful intervention; however, on many sites, participants can simply rejoin under a new name.

A recent effort by the company that hosts the MMOG *League of Legends* suggests that involving the community can be a more effective way of addressing "toxicity," or negative online conduct, at least in the gaming world.[39] The moderators of *League of Legends* developed an online tribunal system in which players are invited to weigh in and decide the fate of players who are reported for disrespect, unsportsmanlike conduct, or outright hate speech. The tribunals have resulted in notable decreases in negative behaviors.

Efforts like these to engage the community in monitoring itself and establishing codes of conduct are promising. Similar practices are part of the culture of other online spaces, such as Reddit, where community dialogue about inappropriate sub-reddits (user-generated forums) has been effective in some respects, even if the dialogue is not always civil. Yet, these efforts require a willingness on the part of technology companies to cede some measure of control and listen to the community.

Educational Fronts

As previously discussed, our interviews with young people and adults pointed to a mentorship gap regarding ethical issues online. Conversations about the Internet are happening at schools, yet the messages that youth get from these conversations are often narrowly focused on personal risks.[40] There may be good, or at least understandable, reasons for this gap. Time constraints in the school day may mean that educators focus their limited time on what they perceive to be the most urgent Internet-related issues. Consequence-oriented messages may then be favored over discussions of ethical issues.

Even when moral and ethical issues appear on the educational agenda, there is no guarantee of a transfer of ethical thinking routines stimulated offline to the ways of thinking youth adopt when they are tweeting, posting content on Tumblr, and updating their Facebook statuses. Schools can prompt moral and ethical sensitivity, but further support is necessary for youth to follow through in practice.

Despite these limitations, I do believe that education has a key role to play in addressing the digital ethics gap. Schools are a significant entry point for reaching large numbers of young people. After-school programs and other sites of informal learning may be even more powerful, given that youth often participate voluntarily in these and thus may be more engaged. With the facilitation of a skilled educator, students can acknowledge and explore the moral and ethical dimensions of online life in generative ways and in concert with the peers with whom they often interact online.

Moreover, peer educators, who often have deeper experience in the online contexts that youth frequent than adults do, can convene youths for reflective conversations about the digital dilemmas they face online. Finally, schools can encourage or even require digital time-outs to facilitate moral and ethical reflection.

For these reasons, my colleagues and I have placed considerable energy into developing activities for use in schools and other learning contexts. With Henry Jenkins and Project New Media Literacies, we developed *Our Space: Being a Responsible Citizen of the Digital World*, a casebook of educational materials for middle and high schools students.[41] Each activity is designed to engage one or more of the ethical thinking skills described above.

The content includes role-playing exercises, creative activities, and prompts for reflection about one's values and sense of responsibility on the Internet. For example, in one role-playing activity, youths are tasked with creating an advertising campaign. As they look at different photographs and other content for their campaigns, they are prompted to ask questions about intellectual property and fair use.

Our research has also informed Common Sense Media's Digital Literacy and Citizenship Curriculum for kindergarten through high school.[42] The curriculum draws on the distinctions among self-focused, moral, and ethical thinking and puts forth a "rings of responsibility" framework. Each ring encourages consideration of a different target—oneself, one's family and friends, and a larger community—when making choices online. These materials are aimed at creating opportunities to consider different perspectives and responsibilities, thus broadening the typically self-focused considerations young people bring to their online decision making.

Throughout our educational efforts, we have aimed not to provide right or wrong answers to the complex dilemmas that surface online but rather to stimulate young people to wrestle with their choices, to see them as dilemmas with moral and ethical significance. The extent to which prompts carried out in a classroom setting actually influence the ways of thinking, sensitivity, and habits of mind assumed when youth are online is unclear. Yet as with the educational tool kits created by my colleagues at the Good Project and Project Zero, such exercises, we believe, can help prepare youth for the dilemmas they may face, both offline and online.[43]

Home Fronts

Like the gap in school-based support, a parental mentorship gap in Internet-related support was evident in our study as well. The data from our interviews with teens and young adults suggested that their parents played only minor roles in their online thinking.[44] When parents did influence youth, either through explicit discussion or implicit modeling, their messages were rarely concerned with ethical issues. The tweens with whom we spoke reported more guidance on the part of their parents. However, the advice the parents gave was almost always about safety issues, "stranger danger," and the negative personal consequences of posting inappropriate content.[45]

Earlier I referred to such parent-youth conversations as missed opportunities, in part because parents should be well-situated to guide their children's attention to moral and ethical concerns. Young people often cite their parents as key figures in their lives to whom they feel responsible, especially when they make important life decisions. Parental figures should thus be poised to influence their children's online ways of thinking, too. To the extent that youth are willing to share aspects of their online lives, parents can identify and help to correct blind spots and disconnects.

Parents can engage their children in thoughtful discussions of actual online situations and encourage them to wrestle with the related moral and ethical questions. Just as parents may do regarding physical schoolyard conflicts, they can nudge their children to exercise empathy, show respect for others, and embody other aspects of moral thinking. They can also remind their children that they are part of larger communities and that their choices can have distant effects, even if they can't be seen directly.

Parents are in a unique position to create and enforce the aforementioned digital time-outs for reflection about these issues. Finally, parents—particularly those who are active online participants themselves—can point out inspiring examples of digital citizenship; in so doing, they may cultivate ethical agency.

There is one more important point to make about the roles of parents, schools, and digital technologies in youth's digital lives. With the help of online search engines, some schools have ventured down the path of surveilling students' online conduct in order to stay apprised of cyberbullying and other problematic online behaviors.[46] Many parents also believe that monitoring their tweens' and teens' text messages, social media and email accounts, and other apps is the best mechanism for keeping their children safe.

As a parent myself, I can appreciate the caring motivations behind such acts. Discovering harmful online exchanges can certainly be an impetus for the kinds of reflective conversations I advocate. Yet I worry about the implications of such surveillance for youth developing the disposition to attend to the issues raised in this book. If adults are always watching, intervening, and thus sensitizing youth to the dilemmas, young people won't be given adequate room to develop conscientious habits of mind of their own. As Henry Jenkins has quipped, "Adults shouldn't be looking over kids' shoulders, but they should have their backs."[47] The recommendations I've suggested in this chapter are made in that spirit.

Peer Fronts

Like adults, peers may encourage and support individualistic modes of thinking above moral and ethical concerns. The desire for peer acceptance and validation may play into blind spots and disconnects—including failures to think past "everybody downloads" and consider potential ethical connotations, and confront mean-spirited online comments. So although peer culture is a critical front on which to address the digital ethics gap, its success hinges on visible acts of digital citizenship on the part of young people.

Although technology companies, teachers, and parents can exert an influence, informal norms set by fellow participants are often more powerful inspiration for good or troubling behavior online. In this book, I have frequently pointed to the powerful role of peers in the choices young people make in new media environments. Peers may include close friends, classmates and other acquaintances, siblings and other young family members, and online-only friends in gaming, blogging, or creative communities.

What these individuals choose to share and say about other people— whether they are kind, concerned, upstanding, and supportive or cruel, dismissive, by-standing, and critical online—helps set the tone of online social networks. How, and to what end, fellow players support one another in a MMOG can affect the moral and ethical choices they make.[48] Attribution practices in blogging and creative communities can establish an atmosphere of respect rather than a fear that one's work will go uncredited.

Although modeling through their online behavior is central, some peers influence other youths in more explicit ways. For example, some tweens talked about their friends or slightly older siblings helping them set up their social network profiles, choose privacy settings, and make decisions about what to share versus hold back online. Among a small number of youths, we found the promising practice of developing social privacy agreements— explicit understandings about what to share about one another online. Some youths described their habit of checking in with friends before sharing specific pieces of content featuring them. As I suggested in chapter 2, explicit conversations among youths about privacy expectations, among other areas of concern, seem essential. Although some youths take the initiative with their friends and peers, parents and teachers can do more to encourage these conversations.

Individual Fronts

Digital affordances and constraints can set the stage; teachers and parents can guide, counsel, and prompt reflection; peers can encourage and inspire specific modes of action, either implicitly or explicitly. But ultimately it is the individual young person who makes sense of the landscape, considers his or her choices and responsibilities, and chooses various courses of action online. The beliefs and values an individual holds—about honesty, respect, responsibility, and what it means to be a good person—can provide an anchor, assuming these moral values are salient to his or her identity and are considered and invoked when a moral or an ethical situation arises.

Another individual factor that appears to be germane is the extent to which a young person is invested in an online activity and thus often a community of practice. As described in chapter 4, young bloggers, creators, and gamers who were deeply invested in their activities showed an inclination for ethical sensitivity in relation to participation-related themes, such as speech and cheating. These "interest-driven" youths felt responsible to and for the integrity of the communities in which they were participants.[49]

Investment certainly does not always coincide with ethics, however; a blogger can be deeply committed to white supremacy and invested in a blogging community that seeks to further this cause. The point is to consider ways to encourage youth to value their online activities, respect their fellow participants, and feel a sense of responsibility to themselves and to a larger community. Adults have an important role to play here. Valuing interest-driven forms of online participation can yield benefits for young people's learning as well, as advocates of the Connected Learning movement argue.[50]

My purpose in this chapter has been to consider the role that these entry points—digital, educational, parental, peer, and individual—have in addressing the ethics gap and promoting more conscientious approaches to online life. Separately, the various fronts may make little progress in closing the digital ethics gap, especially given the particular drawbacks of each that I've acknowledged. Together, though, significant gains may be made. But closing the gap also requires the will and the desire to spend less time on other agendas—Internet safety, for one—in order to focus on ethics and citizenship.

Conclusion: A Bright Spot

My focus in this book has been on the deficits, gaps, disconnects, and blind spots that are evinced all too often, in my view, in our mediated interactions. Yet I have also called attention to the positive aspects of these interactions—examples of both empathetic and ethically sensitive approaches to online life that do exist, though not as often as they should. Moreover, I described a vision of conscientious connectivity that is grounded in moral and ethical thinking skills, sensitivity, motivation, and agency and that is mindful of the challenging dimensions of our interconnected lives. In that spirit, I end this book with a bright spot that underscores the double-edged nature of the Web—the opportunities for both good and evil at our fingertips.

The Steubenville story, along with the other extreme cases described in this book, represents both a horrific offline incident and the worst-case scenario of how social media and the Internet can be used. However, as noted above, the Internet also yields exemplary acts of ethics and social responsibility—and often by young people. The Steubenville case itself inspired something that in my view exemplifies such conscientious approaches to the Web.

In March 2013, University of Oregon student Samantha Stendal, incensed by the wretched details emerging from the Steubenville trial, produced a counternarrative in the form of a short film. Entitled, *A Needed Response*, the 27-second film depicts a young woman passed out on a couch. A young man, speaking directly to the camera, says, "Hey bros. Check who's passed out on the couch. Guess what I'm going to do to her?" He then proceeds to tuck a pillow under her head, cover her with a blanket, and place a glass of water on a table next to her. Turning back to the camera, the young man simply says, "Real men treat women with respect."[51]

Stendal posted this video on YouTube on March 22, 2013. Within two days, it had received nearly 700,000 hits.[52] As of this writing, the video has been viewed nearly 3 million times. The comment thread contains a mix of supportive and disheartening responses. Regardless, the video has captured wide attention.

Stendal's creation touches on key features of conscientious connectivity: sensitivity to the troubling dimensions of the rape case and of the powerful roles that digital technologies and social media played; a motivation to use these media to create a thoughtful response; and agency—the use of her digital camera and of YouTube for a greater good. Set against the blind spots, disconnects, and inhumanity displayed online by the high school boys in Steubenville, this digital artifact persists as a model act of digital citizenship.

I hope that the portrait I've shared in these pages is received as intended: as a nuanced account of the digital ethics gap, attuned to the blind spots and disconnects, but sensitive to the bright spots, too. I also hope that the dilemmas, challenges, and opportunities I've discussed will stay with you. Ideally, they will inform your own thinking about online life, your habits of connectivity, and your conversations with others—especially young people—about the increasingly digital lives we lead.

Appendix: About the Research

The primary data that inform the arguments in this book were collected as part of the Good Play Project, a six-year initiative funded by the John D. and Catherine T. MacArthur Foundation's Digital Media and Learning program.

The Good Play Project was launched with the purpose of investigating young people's ethical sensibilities in relation to the new digital media. Led by Howard Gardner and me as principal investigators and based at Project Zero at the Harvard Graduate School of Education, the project involved a team of 12 other researchers over six years. The following individuals were involved in the project in some capacity: Jessica Benjamin, James Croft, Katie Davis, Andrea Flores, John M. Francis, Sam Gilbert, Erhardt Graeff, Julie Maier, Lindsay Pettingill, Margaret Rundle, Jen Oxman Ryan, and Margaret Weigel.

Our research team began its investigation in 2007 by conducting interviews with 35 informants—individuals with expertise based on studying online life, educating youth with and about technology, or designing online communities. We also interviewed young people who were recognized leaders or highly invested participants in online contexts such as blogs, social networks, and games. Based on these interviews, our team published a monograph, *Young People, Ethics, and the New Digital Media*.[1]

This monograph put forth a framework of five fault lines that we argued are morally and ethically relevant in the digital age: identity, privacy, property (ownership and authorship), credibility, and participation. The current book reconsiders three of these fault lines—privacy, property, and participation—bringing additional data to bear on them. This framework of fault lines anchored our further empirical investigations.

In four years, we conducted three main phases of qualitative data collection with the following populations: tweens, teens and young adults, and "influential adults" in young people's lives (e.g., parents and teachers). During the last year of our project, we conducted a small number of interviews with "young digital citizens," youths involved in efforts to create a more socially responsible Internet.

Phase I

In 2008, our research team conducted interviews with 61 teens and young adults ages 15–25. We recruited youth from high schools, colleges, and work sites and through online communities. We sought to interview young people heavily engaged in different categories of online activity: blogs, social networks, content creation, and gaming. Notably, all youth interviewed were engaged in multiple online activities; however, we chose one context of activity as a key focal point in most interviews. We also sought a sample that was balanced in terms of age subgroups (i.e., high school, college, and postcollege) and diverse in terms of sex, race, and ethnicity. Table A.1 displays the demographic characteristics of this sample and includes the distribution across the different categories of online participation.

Our methods for this phase of the study—as for the other phases—were largely qualitative. We conducted brief preinterview surveys in order to gain preliminary information about participants' time online and specific activities. These surveys also helped us determine eligibility for the interviews. We then conducted two in-depth interviews with each participant.

The first, the "person-centered interview," focused on the participant's experiences and choices online, going back to his or her introduction to the Internet. We collected data on the participants' core online activity; perceptions of peer norms in that context; their influences, mentors, and other sources of guidance; their other uses of the Internet; and their general perceptions of online life. We also asked some general questions about their key offline involvements, influences, and mentors.

In the second interview, the "dilemma interview," we presented each participant with two hypothetical scenarios from a set of five scenarios we devised based on the fault lines of identity, privacy, property (ownership and authorship), credibility, and participation. The scenarios and findings from the privacy, property, and participation dilemmas are featured in this book.

Table A.1
Demographic Characteristics of Teen and Young Adult Sample (*n* = 61)

Age	
Range	15–25 years
Mean	19 years

Age Group	
High school age	20 participants
College age	24
Postcollege age	17

Core Online Activity	
Blogging	13
Content creation	8
Gaming	14
Social networking	26

Sex	
Female	32
Male	29

Race	
Asian	8
Black	8
Native American	1
White	34
Other	10

Ethnicity	
African	4
East Asian	4
European American	26
Latino	4
South Asian	3
Other	12
No response	8

Mother's Education	
Less than high school	3
High school graduate or GED	10
Some college	6
College graduate	16
Graduate or professional degree	19
Don't know or did not report	7

Phase II

In 2010, we conducted interviews with 42 tweens ages 10–14. We recruited participants through middle schools and after-school programs. In this phase of study, we did not seek out youth involved in specific categories of online activity; rather, we merely sought to involve youth who spent a significant amount of time online. We also aimed for a diverse sample in terms of sex, race, and ethnicity. Table A.2 shows the demographic characteristics of this sample.

As in the phase 1 study, we asked each participant to complete a brief preinterview survey in order to establish eligibility and gain background information about participants' online activities that could be probed further in interviews. We interviewed each tween participant twice, as well. Each interview included a mix of person-centered and dilemma questions. We asked tweens about their favorite online activities and digital devices, their experiences and choices online (especially regarding the five fault lines), and the messages they hear from peers, parents, and teachers about online life. We also asked selected questions about their offline activities, mentors, and other influences. We presented each participant with two hypothetical scenarios. One scenario involved copying in an online comics community and was therefore focused on property (ownership and authorship) issues.

The second scenario involved different forms of identity exploration on social networks and touched on various fault lines—including identity, privacy, and participation. For this age group, we used visual materials to make the scenarios as vivid as possible.

Phase III

In 2011, we conducted brief surveys and interviews with 40 "influential adults" in the lives of youth in their tween years. Our sample included educators (e.g., librarians and media specialists), classroom teachers, and parents. After conducting a brief preinterview survey about the participants' own online activities and those of their students and/or children, we interviewed each participant once. The interview protocol consisted of questions parallel to those asked of the young people we interviewed—including lightly adapted dilemmas that mirrored the comic and identity exploration

Table A.2

Demographic Characteristics of Tween Sample (n = 42)

Age	
Range	10–14 years
Mean	12 years
Sex	
Female	24 participants
Male	18

Grade in School	
5th grade	12
6th grade	11
7th grade	9
8th grade	10

Race	
Asian	4
Black	18
White	11
Other	9

Ethnicity	
African	4
European American	2
East Asian	2
Latino	10
South Asian	2
Other	7
No response	15

Mother's Education	
Less than high school	2
High school graduate or GED	7
Some college	6
College graduate	9
Graduate or professional degree	8
Don't know or did not report	10

scenarios posed to tweens. However, we also asked adults pointed questions about the conversations they have with young people about the Internet and digital life in general. Table A.3 shows the demographic characteristics of the adult sample.

Table A.3
Demographic Characteristics of Adult Sample (*n* = 40)

Age	
Range	26–61 years
Mean	43 years

Sex	
Female	29 participants
Male	11

Role	
Educator	14
Classroom teacher	12
Parent	14

Race	
Asian	3
Black	6
White	27
Other	4

Ethnicity	
African	0
East Asian	0
European American	1
Latino	5
South Asian	1
Other	0
No response	33

Education	
High school graduate or GED	1
Some college	2
College graduate	14
Graduate or professional degree	23

Phase IV

In 2012, a member of our research team conducted interviews with eight young people between the ages of 14 and 20 who were nominated based on their possible involvement in "digital literacy and citizenship" efforts—that is, efforts to stem cyberbullying, address privacy issues, develop games and other learning-rich online spaces, and create a socially positive Internet in other ways. The interview protocol contained questions similar to those of our previous studies, along with further questions about their online

Table A.4
Demographic Characteristics of Digital Citizens Sample ($n = 8$)

Age	
Range	14–20 years
Mean	17 years
Gender	
Female	5 participants
Male	3
Race	
Asian	1
Black	3
Native American	1
White	2
Other	1
Ethnicity	
African	1
Latino	1
South Asian	1
Other	2
No response	3
Mother's Education	
High school graduate or GED	1
Some college	2
College graduate	1
Graduate or professional degree	3
Don't know or did not report	1

citizenship activities. Table A.4 shows the demographic characteristics of this sample.

Data Analysis

Data from all phases were explored for *emic* and *etic* themes.[2]

Emic themes emerged inductively from participants' narratives. For example, many participants in the first phase of our research made comments that suggested different degrees of investment in their online activities (e.g., "MySpace is a waste of time" or "Blogging is helping me develop writing skills").

Etic codes were developed based on our interest in the ways of thinking that youth display (e.g., consequence, moral, or ethical) and the five fault lines we set out to investigate: identity, privacy, property (ownership and authorship), credibility, and participation. The data for each phase were examined by two to four researchers, and reliability testing was conducted both informally and with support from NVivo, a qualitative software program.

Notes

Front Matter

1. Neil Postman, *Technopoly: The Surrender of Culture to Technology* (New York: Vintage Books, 1993), 5.

2. Jonathan Safran Foer, "How Not to Be Alone," *New York Times*, June 8, 2013, http://www.nytimes.com/2013/06/09/opinion/sunday/how-not-to-be-alone.html.

1 Morality, Ethics, and Digital Life

1. Associated Press, "Dharun Ravi, Convicted in Webcam Spying, Apologizes Before Going to Jail," *New York Times*, May 29, 2012, http://www.nytimes.com/2012/05/30/nyregion/dharun-ravi-convicted-in-webcam-spying-apologizes-before-going-to-jail.html; Ian Parker, "The Story of a Suicide," *New Yorker*, February 6, 2012, http://www.newyorker.com/reporting/2012/02/06/120206fa_fact_parker.

2. Kate Connolly, "Helene Hegemann: 'There's No Such Thing As Originality, Just Authenticity'," *Guardian*, June 23, 2012, http://www.guardian.co.uk/books/2012/jun/24/helene-hegemann-axolotl-novelist-interview; Randy Kennedy, "The Free-Appropriation Writer," *New York Times*, February 27, 2010, http://www.nytimes.com/2010/02/28/weekinreview/28kennedy.html; Nicholas Kulish, "Author, 17, Says It's 'Mixing,' Not Plagiarism," *New York Times*, February 11, 2010, http://www.nytimes.com/2010/02/12/world/europe/12germany.html.

3. William Glaberson, "On Facebook, N.Y.C. Police Officers Maligned West Indian Paradegoers," *New York Times*, December 5, 2011, http://www.nytimes.com/2011/12/06/nyregion/on-facebook-nypd-officers-malign-west-indian-paradegoers.html; "NYPD Disciplines 17 Cops Who Posted Racist Facebook Comments about West Indian Day Parade," *New York Daily News*, n.d., http://www.nydailynews.com/new-york/nypd-disciplines-17-cops-posted-racist-facebook-comments-west-indian-day-parade-article-1.1142642.

4. Don Tapscott, *Growing Up Digital: The Rise of the Net Generation* (New York: McGraw-Hill, 1999); see also John Palfrey and Urs Gasser, *Born Digital: Understanding the First Generation of Digital Natives* (New York: Basic Books, 2010).

5. Glaberson, "On Facebook."

6. Howard Gardner, *Truth, Beauty, and Goodness Reframed: Educating for the Virtues in the Age of Truthiness and Twitter* (New York: Basic Books, 2012); see also Howard Gardner, *Five Minds for the Future* (Cambridge, MA: Harvard Business Review Press, 2007); and Howard Gardner, "Reinventing Ethics," *New York Times*, September 23, 2012, http://opinionator.blogs.nytimes.com/2012/09/23/reinventing-ethics.

7. Jean Decety, ed., *Empathy: From Bench to Bedside* (Cambridge, MA: MIT Press, 2011); Mary Gordon, *Roots of Empathy: Changing the World Child by Child* (New York: Experiment, 2009); Christian Keysers, *The Empathic Brain: How the Discovery of Mirror Neurons Changes Our Understanding of Human Nature* (Lexington, KY: Social Brain Press, 2011); Jeremy Rifkin, *The Empathic Civilization: The Race to Global Consciousness in a World in Crisis* (New York: J. P. Tarcher, 2009); F. B. M. de Waal, *The Age of Empathy: Nature's Lessons for a Kinder Society* (New York: Three Rivers Press, 2009).

8. Emily Bazelon, *Sticks and Stones: Defeating the Culture of Bullying and Rediscovering the Power of Character and Empathy* (New York: Random House, 2013), http://www.amazon.com/Sticks-Stones-Defeating-Rediscovering-Character/dp/0812992806.

9. David Brooks, "The Limits of Empathy," *New York Times*, September 29, 2011, http://www.nytimes.com/2011/09/30/opinion/brooks-the-limits-of-empathy.html; Gardner, *Truth, Beauty, and Goodness Reframed*.

10. Paul Bloom, "The Baby in the Well: The Case Against Empathy," *New Yorker*, May 20, 2013.

11. James R. Rest, Darcia Narvaez, Muriel J. Bebeau, and Stephen J. Thoma, *Postconventional Moral Thinking: A Neo-Kohlbergian Approach* (Mahwah, NJ: Lawrence Erlbaum, 1999).

12. For a more detailed discussion of this ways-of-thinking framework, see Andrea Flores and Carrie James, "Morality and Ethics behind the Screen: Young People's Perspectives on Digital Life," *New Media & Society*, November 21, 2012.

13. My use of the term *consequence thinking* is distinct from the consequentialist, utilitarian philosophical approach of John Stuart Mill and others that advocates the greatest happiness principle, or the greatest good for the greatest number of people. I use *consequence thinking* to denote a strictly or largely self-focused concern with positive or negative consequences. John Stuart Mill, *Utilitarianism* (Buffalo, NY: Prometheus Books, 1987).

14. This notion of perspective taking resonates with Robert Selman's concept of societal perspective taking. Robert L. Selman, "The Relation of Role Taking to the

Development of Moral Judgment in Children," *Child Development* 42, no. 1 (March 1, 1971): 79–91.

15. Danielle Allen, "Good Citizenship: Understanding Youth Power and Justice in the Digital Age," presentation at the Developing Balanced, Responsible, Caring Youth Conference, Dedham, MA, March 8, 2013, http://casieonline.org/events/pz.

16. William Damon, *The Moral Child: Nurturing Children's Natural Moral Growth* (New York: Free Press, 1990); Lawrence Kohlberg, *The Philosophy of Moral Development*, vol. 1: *Moral Stages and the Idea of Justice* (San Francisco: Harper & Row, 1981); Lawrence Kohlberg, *The Psychology of Moral Development*, vol. 2: *The Nature and Validity of Moral Stages* (San Francisco: Harper & Row, 1984); James R. Rest, *Moral Development: Advances in Research and Theory* (Westport, CT: Praeger, 1986); Rest et al., *Postconventional Moral Thinking*.

17. Kohlberg, *The Philosophy of Moral Development*, vols. 1 and 2.

18. Damon, *The Moral Child*; see also Selman, "The Relation of Role Taking"; and Robert L. Selman, "Level of Social Perspective Taking and the Development of Empathy in Children: Speculations from a Social Cognitive Viewpoint," *Journal of Moral Education* 5, no. 1 (1975): 35–43.

19. Damon, *The Moral Child*.

20. Rest, *Moral Development*; Rest et al., *Postconventional Moral Thinking*; James R. Rest, Darcia Narvaez, Stephen J. Thoma, and Muriel J. Bebeau, "A Neo-Kohlbergian Approach to Morality Research," *Journal of Moral Education* 29, no. 4 (2000): 381–395.

21. David Perkins, Shari Tishman, Ron Ritchhart, Kiki Donis, and Al Andrade, "Intelligence in the Wild: A Dispositional View of Intellectual Traits," *Educational Psychology Review* 12, no. 3 (September 1, 2000): 269–293.

22. Max H. Bazerman and Ann E. Tenbrunsel, *Blind Spots: Why We Fail to Do What's Right and What to Do about It* (Princeton, NJ: Princeton University Press, 2011), 8.

23. Ibid, 8–9.

24. Nicholas Negroponte, *Being Digital* (New York: Vintage Books, 1996).

25. Katie Davis, "Young People's Digital Lives: The Impact of Interpersonal Relationships and Digital Media Use on Adolescents' Sense of Identity," *Computers in Human Behavior* 29, no. 6 (November 2013): 2281–2293; Kaveri Subrahmanyam and Patricia Greenfield, "Online Communication and Adolescent Relationships," *Future of Children* 18, no. 1 (Spring 2008): 119–146; Patti M. Valkenburg and Jochen Peter, "Social Consequences of the Internet for Adolescents: A Decade of Research," *Current Directions in Psychological Science* 18, no. 1 (February 1, 2009): 1–5; Patti M. Valkenburg and Jochen Peter, "Online Communication among Adolescents: An Integrated Model of Its Attraction, Opportunities, and Risks," *Journal of Adolescent Health* 48, no. 2 (February 2011): 121–127.

26. Clay Shirky, *Here Comes Everybody: The Power of Organizing without Organizations* (London: Allen Lane, 2008); Clay Shirky, *Cognitive Surplus: How Technology Makes Consumers into Collaborators* (New York: Penguin Books, 2011); Mizuko Ito, Sonja Baumer, Matteo Bittanti, danah boyd, Rachel Cody, Becky Herr-Stephenson, Heather A. Horst, et al., *Hanging Out, Messing Around, and Geeking Out: Kids Living and Learning with New Media* (Cambridge, MA: MIT Press, 2010); Clive Thompson, *Smarter Than You Think: How Technology Is Changing Our Minds for the Better* (New York: Penguin Press, 2013).

27. Nicholas Carr, *The Shallows: What the Internet Is Doing to Our Brains* (New York: W. W. Norton, 2010); Jaron Lanier, *You Are Not a Gadget: A Manifesto* (New York: Knopf, 2010); see also Sherry Turkle, "Always-On/Always-on-You: The Tethered Self," in *Handbook of Mobile Communication Studies*, ed. James E. Katz (Cambridge, MA: MIT Press, 2008), 121–137; and Sherry Turkle, *Alone Together: Why We Expect More from Technology and Less from Each Other* (New York: Basic Books, 2011).

28. Howard Gardner and Katie Davis, *The App Generation: How Today's Youth Navigate Identity, Intimacy, and Imagination in a Digital World* (New Haven, CT: Yale University Press, 2013); Roger Silverstone, "Proper Distance: Towards an Ethics for Cyberspace," in *Digital Media Revisited: Theoretical and Conceptual Innovations in Digital Domains*, ed. Gunnar Liestol, Andrew Morrison, and Terje Rasmussen (Cambridge, MA: MIT Press, 2003), 469–490.

29. Henry Jenkins, *Confronting the Challenges of Participatory Culture: Media Education for the 21st Century* (Cambridge, MA: MIT Press, 2009).

30. Cathy J. Cohen, Joseph Kahne, Ellen Middaugh, Benjamin Bowyer, and Jon Rogowski, *Participatory Politics: New Media and Youth Political Action*, Youth and Participatory Politics Research Network, 2012, http://ypp.dmlcentral.net/publications; Henry Jenkins, Sam Ford, and Joshua Green, *Spreadable Media: Creating Value and Meaning in a Networked Culture* (New York: New York University Press, 2013); Joseph Kahne, Ellen Middaugh, and Danielle Allen, "Youth, New Media, and the Rise of Participatory Politics," in *From Voice to Influence: Understanding Citizenship in the Digital Age*, ed. Danielle Allen and Jennifer Light (forthcoming).

31. danah boyd, "Why Youth ♥ Social Network Sites: The Role of Networked Publics in Teenage Social Life," in *Youth, Identity, and Digital Media*, ed. David Buckingham (Cambridge, MA: MIT Press, 2008), 119–142; danah boyd, "Social Network Sites As Networked Publics: Affordances, Dynamics, and Implications," in *A Networked Self: Identity, Community, and Culture on Social Network Sites*, ed. Zizi Papacharissi (New York: Routledge, 2011), 39–58, http://www.danah.org/papers.

32. Similarly, Patti Valkenburg and Jochen Peter discuss how online communication affords accessibility to close relations as well as the opportunities to forge new ties. Valkenburg and Peter, "Online Communication among Adolescents."

33. Turkle, "Always-On/Always-on-You"; Turkle, *Alone Together*; Douglas Rushkoff, *Present Shock: When Everything Happens Now* (New York: Current, 2013).

34. Turkle, *Alone Together*; Gardner and Davis, *The App Generation*; Kohlberg, *The Psychology of Moral Development*, vol. 2.

35. Joseph Walther's hyperpersonal computer-mediated communication (CMC) model describes these features as positive affordances. Joseph B. Walther, "Computer-Mediated Communication: Impersonal, Interpersonal, and Hyperpersonal Interaction," *Communication Research* 23, no. 1 (February 1, 1996): 3–43. He argues that "CMC users take advantage of the interface and channel characteristics that CMC offers in a dynamic fashion in order to enhance their relational outcomes." Joseph B. Walther, "Selective Self-Presentation in Computer-Mediated Communication: Hyperpersonal Dimensions of Technology, Language, and Cognition," *Computers in Human Behavior* 23, no. 5 (September 2007): 2540.

36. Silverstone, "Proper Distance," 481.

37. John Suler, "The Online Disinhibition Effect," *Cyberpsychology & Behavior* 7, no. 3 (2004): 321.

38. Jimmy Soni, "The Reason HuffPost Is Ending Anonymous Accounts," *Huffington Post*, August 26, 2013, http://www.huffingtonpost.com/jimmy-soni/why-is-huffpost -ending-an_b_3817979.html?utm_hp_ref=tw.

39. Bazerman and Tenbrunsel, *Blind Spots*, 34–36.

40. Turkle, *Alone Together*, 166.

41. Robert Neelly Bellah, Richard Madsen, William M. Sullivan, Ann Swidler, and Steven M. Tipton, *Habits of the Heart: Individualism and Commitment in American Life* (Berkeley: University of California Press, 2008).

42. William Damon, *The Path to Purpose: Helping Our Children Find Their Calling in Life* (New York: Simon and Schuster, 2008); John E Schlimm, *Stand up! 75 Young Activists Who Rock the World and How You Can, Too!* (Orangevale, CA: Publishing Syndicate, 2013).

43. Jean M. Twenge, *Generation Me: Why Today's Young Americans Are More Confident, Assertive, Entitled—and More Miserable Than Ever Before* (New York: Simon and Schuster, 2006); Jean M. Twenge and W. Keith Campbell, *The Narcissism Epidemic: Living in the Age of Entitlement* (New York: Simon and Schuster, 2010); Sara H. Konrath, Edward H. O'Brien, and Courtney Hsing, "Changes in Dispositional Empathy in American College Students over Time: A Meta-Analysis," *Personality and Social Psychology Review* 15, no. 2 (May 2011): 180–198; Heejung Park, Jean M. Twenge, and Patricia M. Greenfield, "The Great Recession Implications for Adolescent Values and Behavior," *Social Psychological and Personality Science* (July 11, 2013), http://spp .sagepub.com/content/early/2013/07/10/1948550613495419.

44. Wendy Fischman, *Making Good: How Young People Cope with Moral Dilemmas at Work* (Cambridge, MA: Harvard University Press, 2005).

45. Al Baker, "70 Students at Stuyvesant to Retake Exams after Cheating Case," *New York Times*, July 9, 2012, http://www.nytimes.com/2012/07/10/nyregion/70-students-at-stuyvesant-to-retake-exams-after-cheating-case.html; Richard Pérez-Peña, "Harvard Forced Dozens to Leave in Cheating Scandal," *New York Times*, February 1, 2013, http://www.nytimes.com/2013/02/02/education/harvard-forced-dozens-to-leave-in-cheating-scandal.html; David Callahan, *The Cheating Culture: Why More Americans Are Doing Wrong to Get Ahead* (New York: Houghton Mifflin Harcourt, 2007).

46. Christian Smith, Kari Christoffersen, Hilary Davidson, and Patricia Snell Herzog, *Lost in Transition: The Dark Side of Emerging Adulthood* (New York: Oxford University Press, 2011), 59.

47. Emile Durkheim, *The Rules of Sociological Method: And Selected Texts on Sociology and Its Method*, ed. Steven Lukes (New York: Free Press, 1982), 50.

48. A handful of participants in the final digital citizenship study were interviewed via Skype.

49. These five themes were derived from an earlier study our research group conducted, which is reported in Carrie James, Katie Davis, Andrea Flores, John M. Francis, Lindsay Pettingill, Margaret Rundle, and Howard Gardner, *Young People, Ethics, and the New Digital Media: A Synthesis from the Good Play Project* (Cambridge, MA: MIT Press, 2009).

50. I personally conducted about 10 percent of the interviews. During data collection, I was in ongoing dialogue with all members of the research team, hearing the details of interviews conducted and reading their interview notes. Ultimately, I analyzed the verbatim transcripts of all interviews conducted.

51. Lanier, *You Are Not a Gadget.*

52. For a relevant and pointed discussion of the distinction between horizontal, peer-to-peer issues on the one hand and vertical, user–to–social media and security agency concerns on the other, see Ross Douthat, "Your Smartphone Is Watching You," *New York Times*, June 8, 2013, http://www.nytimes.com/2013/06/09/opinion/sunday/douthat-your-smartphone-is-watching-you.html.

2   Privacy

1. Elisabeth Soep, "The Digital Afterlife of Youth-Made Media: Implications for Media Literacy Education," *Comunicar* 19, no. 38 (2012): 93–100.

2. Brian Stetler, "Upending Anonymity: These Days the Web Unmasks Everyone," *New York Times*, June 20, 2011.

3. danah boyd, "Social Network Sites As Networked Publics: Affordances, Dynamics, and Implications," in *A Networked Self: Identity, Community, and Culture on Social Network Sites*, ed. Zizi Papacharissi (New York: Routledge, 2011), http://www.danah.org/papers.

4. Jeffrey Rosen, "The Web Means the End of Forgetting," *New York Times*, July 21, 2010, http://www.nytimes.com/2010/07/25/magazine/25privacy-t2.html.

5. danah boyd and Alice Marwick, "Social Privacy in Networked Publics: Teens' Attitudes, Practices, and Strategies," presentation at the Oxford Internet Institute Decade in Internet Time Symposium, Oxford, UK, September 22, 2011, http://papers.ssrn.com/sol3/papers.cfm?abstract_id=1925128; see also Mary Madden, *Privacy Management on Social Media Sites*, Pew Internet and American Life Project, February 24, 2012, http://pewinternet.org/Reports/2012/Privacy-management-on-social-media.aspx; and Mary Madden, Amanda Lenhart, Sandra Cortesi, Urs Gasser, Maeve Duggan, and Aaron Smith, *Teens, Social Media, and Privacy*, Pew Internet and American Life Project, May 21, 2013, http://www.pewinternet.org/Reports/2013/Teens-Social-Media-And-Privacy.aspx.

6. Madden et al., *Teens, Social Media, and Privacy*. See also danah boyd's discussion of "social steganography" or "hiding in plain sight"—a strategy she found among teens in which their online tweets or status updates may convey a superficial, often benign meaning to one audience, such as parents, yet contain an alternative or deeper meaning for an intended audience of close friends. danah boyd, "Social Steganography: Learning to Hide in Plain Sight," *Apophenia*, Zephoria, August 23, 2010, http://www.zephoria.org/thoughts/archives/2010/08/23/social-steganography-learning-to-hide-in-plain-sight.html; boyd and Marwick, "Social Privacy in Networked Publics."

7. "If you're not on MySpace, you don't exist," said Skylar, age 18, quoted in danah boyd, "Why Youth ♥ Social Network Sites: The Role of Networked Publics in Teenage Social Life," in *Youth, Identity, and Digital Media*, ed. David Buckingham (Cambridge, MA: MIT Press, 2008), 119–142.

8. Duane Buhrmester and Karen Prager, "Patterns and Functions of Self-Disclosure during Childhood and Adolescence," in *Disclosure Processes in Children and Adolescents*, ed. Ken J. Rotenberg, (Cambridge, UK: Cambridge University Press, 1995), 10–56; Mary Jo V. Pugh and Daniel Hart, "Identity Development and Peer Group Participation," *New Directions for Child and Adolescent Development* 1999, no. 84 (1999): 55–70.

9. Katie Davis, "Young People's Digital Lives: The Impact of Interpersonal Relationships and Digital Media Use on Adolescents' Sense of Identity," *Computers in Human Behavior* 29, no. 6 (November 2013): 2281–2293; Susannah Stern, "Producing Sites, Exploring Identities: Youth Online Authorship," in *Youth, Identity, and Digital Media*, ed. David Buckingham, (Cambridge, MA: MIT Press, 2008), 95–117; Kaveri Subrah-

manyam and Patricia Greenfield, "Online Communication and Adolescent Relationships," *Future of Children* 18, no. 1 (Spring 2008): 119–146; Patti M. Valkenburg and Jochen Peter, "Social Consequences of the Internet for Adolescents: A Decade of Research," *Current Directions in Psychological Science* 18, no. 1 (February 1, 2009): 1–5; Patti M Valkenburg and Jochen Peter, "Online Communication among Adolescents: An Integrated Model of Its Attraction, Opportunities, and Risks," *Journal of Adolescent Health* 48, no. 2 (February 2011): 121–127.

10. Margo Gardner and Laurence Steinberg, "Peer Influence on Risk Taking, Risk Preference, and Risky Decision Making in Adolescence and Adulthood: An Experimental Study," *Developmental Psychology* 41, no. 4 (July 2005): 625–635; Laurence Steinberg and Elizabeth S. Scott, "Less Guilty by Reason of Adolescence," *American Psychologist* 58, no. 12 (2003): 1009–1018.

11. John Suler, "The Online Disinhibition Effect," *Cyberpsychology & Behavior* 7, no. 3 (2004): 321–326.

12. Karen Bradley, "Internet Lives: Social Context and Moral Domain in Adolescent Development," *New Directions for Youth Development,* no. 108 (2005): 57–76. Stern, "Producing Sites, Exploring Identities."

13. Miriam J. Metzger and Rebekah Pure, "Privacy Management in Facebook," presentation at the annual convention of the National Communication Association's Human Communication and Technology Division, Chicago, 2009.

14. Sonia Livingstone, "Taking Risky Opportunities in Youthful Content Creation: Teenagers' Use of Social Network Sites for Intimacy, Privacy and Self-Expression," *New Media & Society* 10, no. 3 (2008): 393–411.

15. John Palfrey and Urs Gasser, *Born Digital: Understanding the First Generation of Digital Natives* (New York: Basic Books, 2010), 66.

16. Mark S. Granovetter wrote about "the strength of weak ties" in creating economic opportunities in "The Strength of Weak Ties," *American Journal of Sociology,* 78, no. 3 (1973): 1360–1380. Jonathan Coulson applied the theory to online life, theorizing about the social capital formed through weak ties, although he did not fully address the implications for privacy, in *The Strength of Weak Ties in Online Social Networks* (Saarbrücken, Germany: Lambert Academic Publishing, 2010).

17. Metzger and Pure, "Privacy Management in Facebook."

18. Katie Davis and Carrie James, "Tweens' Conceptions of Privacy Online: Implications for Educators," *Learning, Media and Technology* 38, no. 1 (2013): 4–25.

19. We observed this lack of understanding about privacy settings, or a failure to use them effectively, among 11 teens and young adults (18 percent of that sample) and 8 tweens (20 percent of that sample).

20. Ratan Dey, Yuan Ding, and Keith W. Ross, *The High-School Profiling Attack: How Online Privacy Laws Can Actually Increase Minors' Risk*, Polytechnic Institute of New York University, November 16, 2012, http://research.poly.edu/~ross/HighSchool .pdf.

21. Robert Neelly Bellah, Richard Madsen, William M. Sullivan, Ann Swidler, and Steven M. Tipton, *Habits of the Heart: Individualism and Commitment in American Life* (Berkeley: University of California Press, 2008); Robert Neelly Bellah, Richard Madsen, Steven M. Tipton, William M. Sullivan, and Ann Swidler, *The Good Society* (New York: Vintage Press, 1992); Amitai Etzioni, *The Spirit of Community: The Reinvention of American Society* (New York: Touchstone, 1993); Daphna Oyserman, Heather M. Coon, and Markus Kemmelmeier, "Rethinking Individualism and Collectivism," *Psychological Bulletin* 128, no. 1 (2002): 3–72. For recent data about individualism among young people, see Christian Smith, *Lost in Transition: The Dark Side of Emerging Adulthood* (New York: Oxford University Press, 2011).

22. In some important legal decisions, privacy settings (e.g., friends only) in social networks do not allow for a reasonable expectation of privacy. Facebook status updates intended for and shared with "friends only" have been deemed admissible evidence in certain cases. John G. Browning, *The Lawyer's Guide to Social Networking: Understanding Social Media's Impact on the Law* (Boston: Thomson Reuters Aspatore Books, 2010).

23. Tara Kelly, "Ariane Friedrich, German High Jumper, Outs Stalker on Facebook," *Huffington Post*, April 24, 2012, http://www.huffingtonpost.com/2012/04/24/ariane-friedrich-german-high-jumper_n_1449001.html.

24. Lisa W. Foderaro, "Invasion of Privacy Charges after Death of Tyler Clementi," *New York Times*, September 29, 2010, http://www.nytimes.com/2010/09/30/ nyregion/30suicide.html.

25. Associated Press, "Dharun Ravi, Convicted in Webcam Spying, Apologizes Before Going to Jail," *New York Times*, May 29, 2012, http://www.nytimes.com/2012/05/30/ nyregion/dharun-ravi-convicted-in-webcam-spying-apologizes-before-going-to-jail .html.

26. danah boyd, "Reflecting on Dharun Ravi's Conviction," Zephoria, March 19, 2012, http://www.zephoria.org/thoughts/archives/2012/03/19/dharun-ravi-guilty .html; Barbara Ray, "What the Tragedy of Tyler Clementi Can Teach Us about Digital Citizenship," Commonsense Media, February 16, 2012, http://www .commonsensemedia.org/educators/blog/what-tragedy-tyler-clementi-can-teach-us-about-digital-citizenship; Jean M. Twenge, "Generation Me on Trial," *Chronicle of Higher Education*, March 18, 2012, http://chronicle.com/article/Generation -Me-on-Trial/131246.

27. Victoria R. Brown and E. Daly Vaughn, "The Writing on the (Facebook) Wall: The Use of Social Networking Sites in Hiring Decisions," *Journal of Business and Psy-*

chology 26, no. 2 (June 1, 2011): 219–225; Leslie Kwoh, "Beware: Potential Employers Are Watching You," *Wall Street Journal*, October 29, 2012, http://online.wsj.com/article/SB10000872396390443759504577631410093879278.html. For an overview of the legal implications of social media background checks, see Sherry Sanders, *Privacy Is Dead: The Birth of Social Media Background Checks* (Rochester, NY: Social Science Research Network, 2012), http://papers.ssrn.com/abstract=2020790.

28. Laurence Steinberg and Elizabeth S. Scott, "Less Guilty by Reason of Adolescence," *American Psychologist* 58, no. 12 (2003): 1009–1018.

29. Davis, "Young People's Digital Lives"; Subrahmanyam and Greenfield, "Online Communication and Adolescent Relationships"; Kaveri Subrahmanyam and Patricia M. Greenfield, "Virtual Worlds in Development: Implications of Social Networking Sites," *Journal of Applied Developmental Psychology* 29, no. 6 (November 2008): 417–419; Valkenburg and Peter, "Social Consequences of the Internet for Adolescents"; Valkenburg and Peter, "Online Communication among Adolescents."

30. Madden et al., *Teens, Social Media, and Privacy.*

31. Jenna Wortham, "Facebook Made Me Do It," *New York Times*, June 15, 2013, http://www.nytimes.com/2013/06/16/sunday-review/facebook-made-me-do-it.html.

32. For a more extensive discussion of what tweens report about adult involvement in their online lives, see Davis and James, "Tweens' Conceptions of Privacy Online." For broader trends related to parents' oversight of young people's online lives, see Pamela Paul, "Cyber Parents, Accessing Perhaps, TMI," *New York Times*, May 3, 2013, http://www.nytimes.com/2013/05/05/fashion/cyber-parents-accessing-perhaps-tmi.html.

33. Howard Gardner and Katie Davis, *The App Generation: How Today's Youth Navigate Identity, Intimacy, and Imagination in a Digital World* (New Haven, CT: Yale University Press, 2013); David H. Holtzman, *Privacy Lost: How Technology Is Endangering Your Privacy* (San Francisco: Jossey-Bass, 2006). Holtzman also discusses the societal harm associated with waning privacy in a digital age, with an emphasis on the negative effects of corporate surveillance.

34. "Job Applicants and Social Media: Employers Take 'Eyes Wide Shut' Approach," Minnesota Public Radio, http://minnesota.publicradio.org/display/web/2013/04/06/business/prospective-employees-and-social-media; Rosen, "The Web Means the End of Forgetting."

35. Avner Levin and Patricia Sánchez Abril, "Two Notions of Privacy Online," *Vanderbilt Journal of Entertainment & Technology Law* 11 (2009): 1001–1051.

3   Property

1. A survey conducted by the Pew Internet and American Life Project in May 2010 revealed that 53 percent of American Internet users use Wikipedia to find information—this is 42 percent of all Americans. Kathryn Zickuhr and Lee Rainie, *Wikipedia, Past and Present*, Pew Internet and American Life Project, January 13, 2011, http://pewinternet.org/~/media//Files/Reports/2011/PIP_Wikipedia.pdf.

2. Alison J. Head and Michael B. Eisenberg, "How Today's College Students Use Wikipedia for Course-Related Research," *First Monday* 15, no. 3 (March 1, 2010), http://www.uic.edu/htbin/cgiwrap/bin/ojs/index.php/fm/article/view/2830/2476.

3. Zickuhr and Rainie, *Wikipedia, Past and Present*.

4. A doctoral student on our research team, James Croft, conducted a systematic analysis of responses to this Wikipedia scenario. Croft's coauthored and unpublished manuscript, "Authorship and Ownership in the Digital Sphere" (2011), explores in greater depth the responses of youth, their modes of reasoning about the scenario, and the various factors that appeared to affect their responses, including their understanding of how Wikipedia works.

5. Aaron Swartz, *Guerilla Open Access Manifesto*, July 2008, http://archive.org/stream/GuerillaOpenAccessManifesto/Goamjuly2008_djvu.txt. Tragically, Swartz committed suicide in 2013 as he awaited federal prosecution for computer and wire fraud.

6. Matthew David, *Peer to Peer and the Music Industry: The Criminalization of Sharing* (Los Angeles: Sage, 2010), 9.

7. The Creative Commons movement, http://creativecommons.org/, is an admirable effort to address this problem. Through a range of Creative Commons license options, creators can signal their preferences for how their content is used—including commercial and noncommercial uses, and with or without attribution and modification.

8. Nicholas Negroponte, *Being Digital* (New York: Vintage Books, 1996).

9. Mizuko Ito, Sonja Baumer, Matteo Bittanti, danah boyd, Rachel Cody, Becky Herr-Stephenson, Heather A. Horst, et al., *Hanging Out, Messing Around, and Geeking Out: Kids Living and Learning with New Media* (Cambridge, MA: MIT Press, 2010); Henry Jenkins, *Confronting the Challenges of Participatory Culture: Media Education for the 21st Century* (Cambridge, MA: MIT Press, 2009); Lawrence Lessig, *Free Culture: The Nature and Future of Creativity* (New York: Penguin Books, 2005).

10. Cathy J. Cohen, Joseph Kahne, Ellen Middaugh, Benjamin Bowyer, and Jon Rogowski, *Participatory Politics: New Media and Youth Political Action*, Youth and Participatory Politics Research Network, 2012, http://ypp.dmlcentral.net/publications.

11. For the account of one of the attorneys who defended Alice Randall in this case, see "A Passion for Art and IP," *Duke Law*, Fall 2004, http://web.law.duke.edu/cspd/pdf/jenkins.pdf.

12. Jenkins, *Confronting the Challenges of Participatory Culture.*

13. Henry Jenkins provides an informative overview of the sometimes fraught relationship between Harry Potter fan fiction and the corporate interests that sought to restrain such creative endeavors. Warner Brothers sought to block certain fan sites, claiming copyright infringement, but eventually retreated. Although she was initially flummoxed by the Potter fan fiction phenomenon, Rowling has largely given her blessing to it. Harry Jenkins, "Harry Potter and Media Literacy," in *Convergence Culture: Where Old and New Media Collide* (New York: New York University Press, 2006).

14. Renee R. Hobbs, *Copyright Clarity: How Fair Use Supports Digital Learning* (Thousand Oaks, CA: Corwin, 2010), provides a helpful overview of fair use and transformative use aimed at educators but valuable for a range of audiences. While advocating for greater and less fearful use of copyrighted materials based on fair use, Hobbs acknowledges that certain uses are complicated. She notes that transformative use in particular is "a matter of degree" and, overall, that "context and situation determine how fair use applies" (48).

15. Yochai Benkler, *The Wealth of Networks: How Social Production Transforms Markets and Freedom* (New Haven, CT: Yale University Press, 2006); Lessig, *Free Culture*; Christine Schweidler and Sasha Costanza-Chock, "Piracy," in *Word Matters: Multicultural Perspectives on Information Societies*, ed. Alain Ambrosi, Valerie Peugeot, and Daniel Pimienta (Caen, France: C & F Editions, 2005), http://vecam.org/article694.html; Siva Vaidhyanathan, *Copyrights and Copywrongs: The Rise of Intellectual Property and How It Threatens Creativity* (New York: New York University Press, 2003).

16. Mark Cenite, Benjamin H. Detenber, Andy W.K. Koh, Alvin L.H. Lim, and Ng Ee Soon, "Doing the Right Thing Online: A Survey of Bloggers' Ethical Beliefs and Practices," *New Media & Society* 11, no. 4 (June 1, 2009): 575–597.

17. As observed by Mizuko Ito and colleagues, different genres of online participation have been observed among youth, including friendship-driven activities ("hanging out") and interest-driven activities ("messing around" and "geeking out"). Most youth were found to engage in friendship activities, such as socializing on Facebook, whereas a smaller number (approximately 10 percent) were estimated to be deeply involved in interest-based online forums such as fan fiction and other creative communities. Mizuko Ito, Heather A. Horst, Matteo Bittanti, danah boyd, Becky Herr-Stephenson, Patricia G. Lange, C.J. Pascoe, and Laura Robinson, *Living and Learning with New Media: Summary of Findings from the Digital Youth Project*, November 2008, http://digitalyouth.ischool.berkeley.edu; Ito et al., *Hanging Out, Messing Around, and Geeking Out*; Mark Warschauer and Tina Matuchniak, "New

Technology and Digital Worlds: Analyzing Evidence of Equity in Access, Use, and Outcomes," *Review of Research in Education* 34, no. 1 (2010): 179–225.

18. Sarah Glazer, "Plagiarism and Cheating: Are They Becoming More Acceptable in the Internet Age?," *CQ Researcher* 23, no. 1 (January 4, 2013), http://library.cqpress .com/cqresearcher/cqresrre2013010400.

19. Hongyan Ma, Eric Yong Lu, Sandra Turner, and Guofang Wan, "An Empirical Investigation of Digital Cheating and Plagiarism among Middle School Students," *American Secondary Education* 35, no. 2 (2007): 69–82.

20. Josephson Institute of Ethics, *2012 Report Card on the Ethics of American Youth*, November 20, 2012, http://charactercounts.org/pdf/reportcard/2012/ReportCard -2012-DataTables-HonestyIntegrityCheating.pdf.

21. Donald L. McCabe, Kenneth D. Butterfield, and Linda K. Treviño, *Cheating in College: Why Students Do It and What Educators Can Do about It* (Baltimore, MD: Johns Hopkins University Press, 2012), 69.

22. Randy Kennedy, "The Free-Appropriation Writer," *New York Times*, February 27, 2010, http://www.nytimes.com/2010/02/28/weekinreview/28kennedy.html; see also Nicholas Kulish, "Author, 17, Says It's 'Mixing,' Not Plagiarism," *New York Times*, February 11, 2010, http://www.nytimes.com/2010/02/12/world/europe/12germany .html.

23. Kate Connolly, "Helene Hegemann: 'There's No Such Thing as Originality, Just Authenticity'," *Guardian*, June 23, 2012, http://www.guardian.co.uk/books/2012/ jun/24/helene-hegemann-axolotl-novelist-interview; see also Kennedy, "The Free-Appropriation Writer"; and Kulish, "Author, 17, Says It's 'Mixing,' Not Plagiarism."

24. Susan Debra Blum, "Intertexuality, Authorship, and Plagiarism," in *My Word! Plagiarism and College Culture* (Ithaca, NY: Cornell University Press, 2009), 29–59.

25. Jen Oxman Ryan, "Downloading, Uploading, and Sharing: Tweens' Conceptions of Authorship and Ownership in the Digital Age," *Journal of Children & Media*, under review.

26. Ibid.

27. Andrés Monroy-Hernández, Benjamin Mako Hill, Jazmin Gonzalez-Rivero, and danah boyd, "Computers Can't Give Credit: How Automatic Attribution Falls Short in an Online Remixing Community," in *Proceedings of the SIGCHI Conference on Human Factors in Computing Systems* (New York: ACM, 2011), 3421–3430.

28. This finding exists uneasily alongside another data point: most youth in our study argued that, in general, Wikipedians should *not* be considered authors.

29. "Global Napster Usage Plummets, but New File-Sharing Alternatives Gaining Ground, Reports Jupiter Media Metrix," *EDP Weekly's IT Monitor*, July 23, 2001,

http://www.thefreelibrary.com/GLOBAL+NAPSTER+USAGE+PLUMMETS,+BUT+NE
W+FILE-SHARING+ALTERNATIVES...-a076784518; Neil Strauss, "Record Labels'
Answer to Napster Still Has Artists Feeling Bypassed," *New York Times*, February 18,
2002,   http://www.nytimes.com/2002/02/18/arts/record-labels-answer-to-napster
-still-has-artists-feeling-bypassed.html?pagewanted=all&src=pm.

30. A helpful discussion of industry efforts to stem piracy and the promising potential of sites like iTunes can be found in John Palfrey and Urs Gasser, *Born Digital:
Understanding the First Generation of Digital Natives* (New York: Basic Books, 2010).

31. American Assembly, *Copyright Infringement and Enforcement in the US: A Research
Note* Columbia University, November 2011, http://piracy.americanassembly.org/
wp-content/uploads/2011/11/AA-Research-Note-Infringement-and-Enforcement
-November-2011.pdf.

32. Swartz, *Guerilla Open Access Manifesto*; see also the Free Culture Foundation,
http://freeculture.org.

33. Shoshana Altschuller and Raquel Benbunan-Fich, "Is Music Downloading the
New Prohibition? What Students Reveal through an Ethical Dilemma," *Ethics and
Information Technology* 11, no. 1 (2009): 49–56; Xiao Wang and Steven R. McClung,
"Toward a Detailed Understanding of Illegal Digital Downloading Intentions: An
Extended Theory of Planned Behavior Approach," *New Media & Society* 13, no. 4
(June 1, 2011): 663–677.

34. When we spoke with the youths about piracy, we were careful to couch our
questions in nonjudgmental ways. We often reminded them that their comments
were confidential and that if the comments were shared, they would be unidentified. Overall, we found the youths to be frank about their involvement in and attitudes about illegal downloading.

35. Palfrey and Gasser, *Born Digital*, 137.

36. Ryan, "Downloading, Uploading, and Sharing." Similarly, 13 percent of the
tweens we interviewed mentioned that a parent, an older sibling, or a cousin downloaded content for them and that they themselves were unaware of the source of the
files.

37. In the 1950s, sociologists Gresham M. Sykes and David Matza described the
neutralization techniques used by "delinquents," or individuals engaged in criminal
or unethical activities. Sykes and Matza's theory is relevant to the ways in which the
youths who indicated that piracy may be ethically problematic justified their decisions to engage in it nonetheless. Gresham M. Sykes and David Matza, "Techniques
of Neutralization: A Theory of Delinquency," *American Sociological Review* 22, no. 6
(December 1957): 664.

Thomas M. Jones's more recent model of "moral intensity" provides additional
support in identifying the common characteristics that affect the extent to which an

issue is granted moral significance. These characteristics are proximity, magnitude of consequences, and concentration of effect. Thomas M. Jones, "Ethical Decision Making by Individuals in Organizations: An Issue-Contingent Model," *Academy of Management Review* 16, no. 2 (April 1991): 366–395.

38. Altschuller and Benbunan-Fich, "Is Music Downloading the New Prohibition?," 53.

39. Oliver Freestone and Vincent-Wayne Mitchell, "Generation Y Attitudes towards e-Ethics and Internet-Related Misbehaviours," *Journal of Business Ethics* 54, no. 2 (2004): 121–128; Aron M. Levin, Mary Conway Dato-On, and Kenneth Rhee, "Money for Nothing and Hits for Free: The Ethics of Downloading Music from Peer-to-Peer Web Sites," *Journal of Marketing Theory & Practice* 12, no. 1 (Winter 2004): 48–60; Robert Siegfried, "Student Attitudes on Software Piracy and Related Issues of Computer Ethics," *Ethics and Information Technology* 6, no. 4 (2004): 215–222.

40. Chun-Yao Huang, "File Sharing as a Form of Music Consumption," *International Journal of Electronic Commerce* 9, no. 4 (Summer 2005): 37–55; Levin, Dato-On, and Rhee, "Money for Nothing and Hits for Free"; Palfrey and Gasser, *Born Digital*.

41. Dawn Poole, "A Study of Beliefs and Behaviors regarding Digital Technology," *New Media & Society* 9, no. 5 (October 1, 2007): 771–793.

42. Certainly, digital forms of content—infinitely copyable as they are—are not met with the problem of scarcity that limits physical artifacts. David, *Peer to Peer and the Music Industry*.

43. McCabe, Butterfield, and Treviño, *Cheating in College*; Jason M. Stephens, Michael F. Young, and Thomas Calabrese, "Does Moral Judgment Go Offline When Students Are Online? A Comparative Analysis of Undergraduates' Beliefs and Behaviors Related to Conventional and Digital Cheating," *Ethics & Behavior* 17, no. 3 (2007): 233–254.

44. Ryan, "Downloading, Uploading, and Sharing."

45. Hobbs, *Copyright Clarity*, 15–38.

46. Levin, Dato-On, and Rhee, "Money for Nothing and Hits for Free."

47. Ma et al., "An Empirical Investigation of Digital Cheating and Plagiarism among Middle School Students"; McCabe, Butterfield, and Treviño, *Cheating in College*; Stephens, Young, and Calabrese, "Does Moral Judgment Go Offline When Students Are Online?"

48. Howard Gardner, "When Ambition Trumps Ethics," *Washington Post*, September 3, 2012, http://www.washingtonpost.com/opinions/when-ambition-trumps-ethics /2012/08/31/495c694a-f384-11e1-892d-bc92fee603a7_story.html; Vivian Yee, "Stuyvesant Students Describe Rationale for Cheating," *New York Times*, September

25, 2012, http://www.nytimes.com/2012/09/26/education/stuyvesant-high-school-students-describe-rationale-for-cheating.html.

49. Jessica K. Parker, "Critical Literacy and the Ethical Responsibilities of Student Media Production," *Journal of Adolescent & Adult Literacy* 56, no. 8 (2013): 668–676.

4   Participation

1. *World of Warcraft* is reported to have had 12 million subscribers at its peak in 2010. In September 2012, *Wired* magazine reported that the game had "lost its cool," because its subscriber base had recently dropped to 9.1 million, still an impressive number. "*World of Warcraft* Has Lost Its Cool," *Wired*, September 2012, http://www.wired.com/gamelife/2012/09/mists-of-pandaria.

2. Dorothy E. Warner and Mike Raiter, "Social Context in Massively-Multiplayer Online Games (MMOGs): Ethical Questions in Shared Space," *International Review of Information Ethics* 4, no. 7 (2005): 46–52.

3. Mia Consalvo, "Rule Sets, Cheating, and Magic Circles: Studying Games and Ethics," *International Review of Information Ethics* 4 (2005): 7–12.

4. Johan Huizinga, *Homo Ludens: A Study of the Play-Element in Culture* (Boston: Beacon Press, 1971).

5. Consalvo, "Rule Sets, Cheating, and Magic Circles."

6. Warner and Raiter, "Social Context in Massively-Multiplayer Online Games (MMOGs)," 47.

7. James Fletcher, "Sexual Harassment in the World of Video Gaming," BBC, June 3, 2012, http://www.bbc.co.uk/news/magazine-18280000; Jason Ocampo, "EVE Online Bank Scandal," *Imagine Games Network*, July 9, 2009, http://www.ign.com/articles/2009/07/09/eve-online-bank-scandal.

8. The developers of *League of Legends*, a multiplayer online game, have developed and tested an array of strategies for reducing griefing and other forms of toxicity in the game. They report success with strategies that empower the game community to adjudicate complaints about negative player behavior. Jeffrey Lin and Carl Kwoh, "Play Nice! The Science of Player Behavior in Online Games," MIT Game Lab, March 20, 2013, http://gamelab.mit.edu/event/play-nice-the-science-of-player-behavior-in-online-games.

9. For a more detailed analysis of responses to the game scenario and related factors, see James Croft, Andrea Flores, John M. Francis, and Sam Gilbert, *"It's Just a Game": Ethical Reasoning in Virtual Worlds*, Project Zero, Harvard Graduate School of Education, 2011, http://www.goodworkproject.org/wp-content/uploads/2011/03/73-Its-Just-a-Game.pdf.

10. Dennis Wrong, *The Problem of Order: What Unites and Divides Society* (Cambridge, MA: Harvard University Press, 1995). Wrong provides a cogent synthesis of sociological and philosophical theories related to this tension and the broader "problem of order" in human societies. Early in the book, he states, "Individuals often feel their attachments and obligations to others as a burden, a painful constraint preventing them from pursuing desires and interests of their own. Indeed, the choice of duty over self-interest or impulse, of the normatively desirable over the actually desired, was defined by Kant as the very essence of moral conduct" (3).

11. Cathy J. Cohen, Joseph Kahne, Ellen Middaugh, Benjamin Bowyer, and Jon Rogowski, *Participatory Politics: New Media and Youth Political Action*, Youth and Participatory Politics Research Network, 2012, http://ypp.dmlcentral.net/publications; Henry Jenkins, *Confronting the Challenges of Participatory Culture: Media Education for the 21st Century* (Cambridge, MA: MIT Press, 2009); Joseph Kahne, Ellen Middaugh, and Danielle Allen, "'Youth, New Media, and the Rise of Participatory Politics,'" in *From Voice to Influence: Understanding Citizenship in the Digital Age*, ed. Danielle Allen and Jennifer Light, forthcoming; Clay Shirky, *Here Comes Everybody: The Power of Organizing without Organizations* (London: Allen Lane, 2008).

12. Jane McGonigal, *Reality Is Broken: Why Games Make Us Better and How They Can Change the World* (New York: Penguin Books, 2011).

13. Itai Himelboim, Stephen McCreery, and Marc Smith, "Birds of a Feather Tweet Together: Integrating Network and Content Analyses to Examine Cross-Ideology Exposure on Twitter," *Journal of Computer-Mediated Communication* 18, no. 2 (2013): 40–60; Andrew Keen, *Digital Vertigo: How Today's Online Social Revolution Is Dividing, Diminishing, and Disorienting Us* (New York: St. Martin's Press, 2012); Cass R. Sunstein, *Republic.com 2.0* (Princeton, NJ: Princeton University Press, 2009); Sherry Turkle, *Alone Together: Why We Expect More from Technology and Less from Each Other* (New York: Basic Books, 2011); John Paul Titlow, "#Me: Instagram Narcissism and the Scourge of the Selfie," *ReadWrite*, January 31, 2013, http://readwrite.com/2013/01/31/instagram-selfies-narcissism.

14. For a relevant discussion of "app-enabling" versus "app-dependent" approaches to digital life, see Howard Gardner and Katie Davis, *The App Generation: How Today's Youth Navigate Identity, Intimacy, and Imagination in a Digital World* (New Haven, CT: Yale University Press, 2013).

15. David Segal, "Closed in Error on Google Places, Merchants Seek Fixes," *New York Times*, September 5, 2011, http://www.nytimes.com/2011/09/06/technology/closed-in-error-on-google-places-merchants-seek-fixes.html.

16. Mike Blumenthal, "News Flash: Google Mt View Reported Closed!," *Understanding Google Places & Local Search*, August 15, 2011, http://blumenthals.com/blog/2011/08/15/google-mt-view-reported-closed.

17. David Streitfeld, "Yelp Tries to Halt Deceptive Reviews," *New York Times*, October 18, 2012, http://www.nytimes.com/2012/10/18/technology/yelp-tries-to-halt -deceptive-reviews.html.

18. "R. J. Ellory, Author, Caught Writing Fake Amazon Reviews for Books," *Huffington Post*, September 4, 2012, http://www.huffingtonpost.com/2012/09/04/rj-ellory -fake-amazon-reviews-caught_n_1854713.html; Christina Ng, "Writer Caught Faking Amazon Reviews," ABC News, September 3, 2012, http://abcnews.go.com/ International/crime-writer-rj-ellory-caught-faking-amazon-reviews/story?id =17143005.

19. Greg Lukianoff, "Twitter, Hate Speech, and the Costs of Keeping Quiet," CNET, n.d., http://news.cnet.com/8301-1023_3-57578140-93/twitter-hate-speech-and-the -costs-of-keeping-quiet/; Jeffrey Rosen, "The Deciders: The Future of Privacy and Free Speech in the Age of Facebook and Google," *Fordham Law Review* 80, no. 4 (March 19, 2012): 1525; Jeffrey Rosen, "The Delete Squad: Google, Twitter, Facebook and the New Global Battle over the Future of Free Speech," *New Republic*, April 29, 2013, http://www.newrepublic.com/article/113045/free-speech-internet-silicon-valley -making-rules#; Somini Sengupta, "On Web, a Fine Line on Free Speech across the Globe," *New York Times*, September 16, 2012, http://www.nytimes.com/2012/09/17/ technology/on-the-web-a-fine-line-on-free-speech-across-globe.html.

20. Elisabeth Soep, "The Digital Afterlife of Youth-Made Media: Implications for Media Literacy Education," *Comunicar* 19, no. 38 (2012): 93–100.

21. Ad Council, *"Think Before You Post" PSA Campaign*, March 23, 2007, http:// multivu.prnewswire.com/mnr/adcouncil/26474.

22. Eli Dresner and Susan C. Herring, "Functions of the Nonverbal in CMC: Emoticons and Illocutionary Force," *Communication Theory* 20, no. 3 (2010): 249–268; J. L. Austin, *How to Do Things with Words*, ed. J. O. Urmson and Marina Sbisà, 2nd ed. (Cambridge, MA: Harvard University Press, 1975).

23. Joseph B. Walther, Jeffrey F. Anderson, and David W. Park, "Interpersonal Effects in Computer-Mediated Interaction: A Meta-Analysis of Social and Antisocial Communication," *Communication Research* 21, no. 4 (August 1, 1994): 460–487.

24. danah boyd uses the terms "social steganography" and "hiding in plain sight" to describe how teens' online status updates may convey a superficial, often benign meaning to a particular audience, such as parents, and an alternative or deeper meaning to close friends. boyd's finding reveals how youth are developing sophisticated strategies for managing privacy and the unintended audience problem on the web. danah boyd, "Social Steganography: Learning to Hide in Plain Sight," *Apophenia*, Zephoria, August 23, 2010, http://www.zephoria.org/thoughts/archives/2010 /08/23/social-steganography-learning-to-hide-in-plain-sight.html; danah boyd and Alice Marwick, "Social Privacy in Networked Publics: Teens' Attitudes, Practices, and Strategies," presentation at the Oxford Internet Institute Decade in Internet Time

Symposium, Oxford, UK, September 22, 2011, http://papers.ssrn.com/sol3/papers
.cfm?abstract_id=1925128.

This phenomenon also echoes findings from historian James Scott's studies of
oppressed groups' use of "hidden transcripts," often embedded in song, to share
information and build solidarity in plain sight of oppressors. James C. Scott, *Domi-
nation and the Arts of Resistance: Hidden Transcripts* (New Haven, CT: Yale University
Press, 1992).

25. "Vaguebooking," *Urban Dictionary*, http://www.urbandictionary.com/define
.php?term=Vaguebooking.

26. Gregory Ferenstein, "Study: Facebook Comments Are More Civil Than Newspa-
per Website Comments," *TechCrunch*, October 13, 2013, http://techcrunch
.com/2013/10/13/study-facebook-comments-are-more-civil-than-newspaper-
website-comments/; Ian Rowe, "Civility 2.0: A Comparative Analysis of Incivility in
Online Political Discussion," presentation at the Elections, Public Opinion, and Parties Conference, University of Lancaster, UK, September 14, 2013, http://www
.lancaster.ac.uk/fass/events/epop2013/docs/Rowe_Civility_2%200_EPOPpdf.pdf.

27. Judith S. Donath, "Identity and Deception in the Virtual Community," in *Communities in Cyberspace*, ed. Peter Kollock and Marc Smith (London: Routledge, 1999),
29–59; Susan Herring, Kirk Job-Sluder, Rebecca Scheckler, and Sasha Barab, "Searching for Safety Online: Managing 'Trolling' in a Feminist Forum," *Information Society*
18, no. 5 (2002): 371–384; Patricia G. Lange, "Commenting on Comments: Investigating Responses to Antagonism on YouTube," presentation at the Society for
Applied Anthropology Conference, Tampa, FL, April 17, 2007, http://sfaapodcasts
.files.wordpress.com/2007/04/update-apr-17-lange-sfaa-paper-2007.pdf; Peter J. Moor,
"Conforming to the Flaming Norm in the Online Commenting Situation," June 29,
2007, http://scholar.petermoor.nl/flaming.pdf; Peter J. Moor, Ard Heuvelman, and
Ria Verleur, "Flaming on YouTube," *Computers in Human Behavior* 26, no. 6 (November 2010): 1536–1546; Patrick B. O'Sullivan and Andrew J. Flanagin, "Reconceptual-
izing 'Flaming' and Other Problematic Messages," *New Media & Society* 5, no. 1
(March 1, 2003): 69–94; Walther, Anderson, and Park, "Interpersonal Effects in
Computer-Mediated Interaction."

28. Peter J. Moor and colleagues have conducted various studies on the incidence,
perception, and effects of flaming on online participants. They find support for the
social psychological processes of deindividuation and depersonalization in anonymous online contexts; these processes result in "conformation to perceived group
norms." Moor et al., "Flaming on YouTube," 1537; see also Moor, "Conforming to
the Flaming Norm."

29. Nancy Baym, *Personal Connections in the Digital Age* (Malden, MA: Polity, 2010);
Howard Rheingold, *The Virtual Community: Homesteading on the Electronic Frontier*
(Cambridge, MA: MIT Press, 2000); Shelly Rodgers and Qimei Chen, "Internet Com-

munity Group Participation: Psychosocial Benefits for Women with Breast Cancer," *Journal of Computer-Mediated Communication* 10, no. 4 (2005).

30. Maria Konnikova, "The Psychology of Online Comments," *New Yorker*, October 24, 2013, http://www.newyorker.com/online/blogs/elements/2013/10/the-psychology -of-online-comments.html?utm_source=tny&utm_campaign= generalsocial &utm_ medium=twitter; Suzanne LaBarre, "Why We're Shutting Off Our Comments," *Popular Science*, September 2013, http://www.popsci.com/science/article/2013-09/ why-were-shutting-our-comments; Sarah Sobieraj, "Let's Not Feed the Trolls—but Let's Not Starve Online Comments, Either," *Cognoscenti*, WBUR, October 24, 2013, http://cognoscenti.wbur.org/2013/10/24/no-comment-sarah-sobieraj; Jimmy Soni, "The Reason HuffPost Is Ending Anonymous Accounts," *Huffington Post*, August 26, 2013, http://www.huffingtonpost.com/jimmy-soni/why-is-huffpost-ending-an_b_381 7979.html?utm_hp_ref=tw.

31. Lee Rainie, *The Tone of Life on Social Networking Sites*, Pew Internet and American Life Project, February 9, 2012, http://pewinternet.org/Reports/2012/Social- networking-climate.aspx; Amanda Lenhart, Mary Madden, Aaron Smith, Kristen Purcell, Kathryn Zickuhr, and Lee Rainie, *Teens, Kindness and Cruelty on Social Network Sites*, November 9, 2011, http://pewinternet.org/Reports/2011/Teens-and -social-media/Summary/Findings.aspx.

32. Knowledge Networks, *Associated Press–MTV Digital Abuse Study*, August 2011, http://www.athinline.org/pdfs/MTV-AP_2011_Research_Study-Exec_Summary.pdf; Victoria Rideout, *Social Media, Social Life: How Teens View Their Digital Lives*, Common Sense Media, June 26, 2012, http://www.commonsensemedia.org/research /social-media-social-life.

33. VitalSmarts, "Antisocial Networks: Hostility on Social Media Rising for 78 Percent of Users," April 10, 2013, http://www.vitalsmarts.com/press/2013/04/antisocial -networks-hostility-on-social-media-rising-for-78-percent-of-users.

34. Mary Madden, Amanda Lenhart, Sandra Cortesi, Urs Gasser, Maeve Duggan, and Aaron Smith, *Teens, Social Media, and Privacy*, Pew Internet and American Life Project, May 21, 2013, http://www.pewinternet.org/Reports/2013/Teens-Social- Media-And-Privacy.aspx.

35. Karen Bradley, "Internet Lives: Social Context and Moral Domain in Adolescent Development," *New Directions for Youth Development*, no. 108 (2005): 57–76; Katie Davis, "Coming of Age Online: The Developmental Underpinnings of Girls' Blogs," *Journal of Adolescent Research* 25, no. 1 (January 1, 2010): 145–171; Katie Davis, "Tensions of Identity in a Networked Era: Young People's Perspectives on the Risks and Rewards of Online Self-Expression," *New Media & Society* (November 8, 2011): ; Katie Davis, "Young People's Digital Lives: The Impact of Interpersonal Relationships and Digital Media Use on Adolescents' Sense of Identity," *Computers in Human Behavior* 29, no. 6 (November 2013): 2281–2293; Kaveri Subrahmanyam and Patricia M.

Greenfield, "Virtual Worlds in Development: Implications of Social Networking Sites," *Journal of Applied Developmental Psychology* 29, no. 6 (November 2008): 417–419; Sherry Turkle, *Life on the Screen: Identity in the Age of the Internet* (New York: Simon & Schuster, 1997); Patti M. Valkenburg and Jochen Peter, "Social Consequences of the Internet for Adolescents: A Decade of Research," *Current Directions in Psychological Science* 18, no. 1 (February 1, 2009): 1–5; Patti M. Valkenburg and Jochen Peter, "Online Communication among Adolescents: An Integrated Model of Its Attraction, Opportunities, and Risks," *Journal of Adolescent Health* 48, no. 2 (February 2011): 121–127.

36. Brian Stelter, "Upending Anonymity, These Days the Web Unmasks Everyone," *New York Times*, June 20, 2011, http://www.nytimes.com/2011/06/21/us/21anony mity.html.

37. Davis, "Coming of Age Online"; Davis, "Tensions of Identity in a Networked Era." Other scholars who have offered accounts of self-expression and identity online are danah boyd, "Why Youth ♥ Social Network Sites: The Role of Networked Publics in Teenage Social Life," in *Youth, Identity, and Digital Media*, ed. David Buckingham (Cambridge, MA: MIT Press, 2008), 119–142; Sonia Livingstone, "Taking Risky Opportunities in Youthful Content Creation: Teenagers' Use of Social Networking Sites for Intimacy, Privacy and Self-Expression," *New Media & Society* 10, no. 3 (June 1, 2008): 393–411; Zizi Papacharissi, ed., *A Networked Self: Identity, Community, and Culture on Social Network Sites* (New York: Routledge, 2010).

38. David Buckingham, "Introducing Identity," in *Youth, Identity, and Digital Media*, ed. David Buckingham (Cambridge, MA: 2011): 1–22; Erik H. Erikson, *Identity: Youth and Crisis* (New York: W. W. Norton, 1968); Sherry Turkle, "Looking toward Cyberspace: Beyond Grounded Sociology," *Contemporary Sociology* 28, no. 6 (November 1999): 643–648.; Sherry Turkle, "Our Split Screens," in *Community in the Digital Age: Philosophy and Practice*, ed. Andrew Feenberg and Darin Barney (Lanham, MD: Rowman and Littlefield, 2004), 101–117.

39. boyd, "Why Youth ♥ Social Network Sites"; boyd, "Social Steganography: Learning to Hide in Plain Sight"; Madden et al., *Teens, Social Media, and Privacy*.

40. For an in-depth analysis of the hypothetical speech scenarios presented to tweens, see Erhardt Graeff, *Tweens, Cyberbullying, and Moral Reasoning: Separating the Upstanders from the Bystanders*, Project Zero, Harvard Graduate School of Education, 2012, http://thegoodproject.org/wp-content/uploads/2012/09/76-Tweens-Cyber bullying-And-Moral-Reasoning.pdf.

41. boyd, "Why Youth ♥ Social Network Sites."

42. Marshall McLuhan, *Understanding Media: The Extensions of Man* (New York: McGraw-Hill, 1965).

43. Davis, "Tensions of Identity in a Networked Era," 11.

44. The most common response to this online speech scenario was concern that the perpetrator would get into trouble, followed by moral concern for the target. The tweens' responses to this scenario stand in notable contrast to the more ethically sensitive responses we observed among more than half of them when we asked how they would feel about a racial or religious group being targeted online. See also Graeff, *Tweens, Cyberbullying, and Moral Reasoning.*

45. Lenhart et al., *Teens, Kindness and Cruelty on Social Network Sites.*

46. Knowledge Networks, *Associated Press–MTV Digital Abuse Study.*

47. Josh Einiger, "Cadaver Photo Comes Back to Haunt Resident," ABC, February 2, 2010, http://abclocal.go.com/wabc/story?section=news/local&id=7253275.

48. Kelly Heyboer, "Medical Students' Cadaver Photos Gets Scrutiny After Images Show Up Online," *Star-Ledger*, March 26, 2010, http://www.nj.com/news/index .ssf/2010/03/medical_schools_examine_ethics.html.

49. Steven Greenhouse, "Employers' Social Media Policies Come under Regulatory Scrutiny," *New York Times*, January 21, 2013, http://www.nytimes.com/2013/01/22/ technology/employers-social-media-policies-come-under-regulatory-scrutiny.html; Jonathan Stempel, "Facebook 'Like' Deserves Free Speech Protection: U.S. Court," Reuters, September 18, 2013, http://www.reuters.com/article/2013/09/18/net-us -usa-speech-facebook-idUSBRE98H0X620130918.

50. Sarah Sobieraj, "Steubenville: 'Digital Residue' of Sexual Assault Lifts Veil on Rape Culture," *Cognoscenti*, WBUR, March 12, 2013, http://cognoscenti.wbur .org/2013/03/12/steubenville-sarah-sobieraj.

51. The facts surrounding the 1964 Kitty Genovese murder and the lack of response by 38 neighbors have recently been questioned. See Leslie Kaufman, "Releasing Old Nonfiction Books When Facts Have Changed," *New York Times*, January 30, 2013, http://www.nytimes.com/2013/01/31/books/releasing-old-nonfiction-books-when -facts-have-changed.html.

52. John Suler, "The Online Disinhibition Effect," *Cyberpsychology & Behavior* 7, no. 3 (2004): 321–326.

53. Danielle Keats Citron and Helen L. Norton, *Intermediaries and Hate Speech: Fostering Digital Citizenship for Our Information Age* (Rochester, NY: Social Science Research Network, 2011), http://papers.ssrn.com/abstract=1764004.

54. Lenhart et al., *Teens, Kindness and Cruelty on Social Network Sites.*

55. Tim Bradshaw, Gerrit Wiesmann, and Robert Cookson, "Twitter Faces Free Speech Dilemma," *Financial Times*, October 18, 2012, http://www.ft.com/intl/cms/s/0 /1e47e772-1943-11e2-af4e-00144feabdc0.html#axzz2WU78rQvs; "Facebook's Online Speech Rules Keep Users On A Tight Leash," *All Things Considered*, NPR, April 3, 2013,

http://www.npr.org/blogs/alltechconsidered/2013/04/03/176147408/facebooks
-online-speech-rules-keep-users-on-a-tight-leash; Rosen, "The Deciders."

56. Lukianoff, "Twitter, Hate Speech, and the Costs of Keeping Quiet"; Audrey Watters, "The Comments Are Closed," *Hack Education*, May 16, 2013, http://www
.hackeducation.com/2013/05/16/the-comments-are-closed. Watters, a technology blogger, recently decided to remove the comments function from her blog after suffering years of sexist abuse. Scholars have shown the extent to which marginalized groups in particular are targeted with hate on the Web. For a comprehensive overview of cyber civil rights issues, see Danielle Keats Citron, *Cyber Civil Rights* (Rochester, NY: Social Science Research Network, 2008), http://papers.ssrn.com/abstract=1271900.

57. Adrian Chen, "Unmasking Reddit's Violentacrez, the Biggest Troll on the Web," *Gawker*, n.d., http://gawker.com/5950981/unmasking-reddits-violentacrez-the
-biggest-troll-on-the-web.

58. William Glaberson, "On Facebook, N.Y.C. Police Officers Maligned West Indian Paradegoers," *New York Times*, December 5, 2011, http://www.nytimes.com
/2011/12/06/nyregion/on-facebook-nypd-officers-malign-west-indian-paradegoers
.html.

59. Danielle Allen discusses the risks that accompany the Internet, where our actions are potentially "boundless" and can come back to haunt us. Danielle Allen, "Good Citizenship: Understanding Youth Power and Justice in the Digital Age," presentation at the Developing Balanced, Responsible, Caring Youth Conference, Dedham, MA, March 8, 2013, http://casieonline.org/events/pz.

60. Ethan Zuckerman, *Rewire: Digital Cosmopolitans in the Age of Connection* (New York: W. W. Norton, 2013).

61. Graeff, *Tweens, Cyberbullying, and Moral Reasoning*.

62. McGonigal, *Reality Is Broken*; Shirky, *Here Comes Everybody*.

5   Correcting the Blind Spots, Reconnecting the Disconnects

1. Richard A. Oppel Jr., "2 Teenagers Found Guilty in Steubenville, Ohio, Rape," *New York Times*, March 17, 2013, http://www.nytimes.com/2013/03/18/us/
teenagers-found-guilty-in-rape-in-steubenville-ohio.html; Juliet Macur and Nate Schweber, "Rape Case Unfolds Online and Divides Steubenville," *New York Times*, December 16, 2012, http://www.nytimes.com/2012/12/17/sports/high-school
-football-rape-case-unfolds-online-and-divides-steubenville-ohio.html.

2. Sarah Sobieraj, "Steubenville: 'Digital Residue' of Sexual Assault Lifts Veil on Rape Culture," *Cognoscenti*, WBUR, March 12, 2013, http://cognoscenti.wbur.org/2013
/03/12/steubenville-sarah-sobieraj.

3. Elisabeth Soep, "The Digital Afterlife of Youth-Made Media: Implications for Media Literacy Education," *Comunicar* 19, no. 38 (2012): 93–100.

4. Paul Bloom, "The Baby in the Well: The Case against Empathy," *New Yorker*, May 20, 2013, http://www.newyorker.com/arts/critics/atlarge/2013/05/20/130520crat _atlarge_bloom.

5. Danielle Allen, "Good Citizenship: Understanding Youth Power and Justice in the Digital Age," presentation at the Developing Balanced, Responsible, Caring Youth Conference, Dedham, MA, March 8, 2013, http://casieonline.org/events/pz; Max H. Bazerman and Ann E. Tenbrunsel, *Blind Spots: Why We Fail to Do What's Right and What to Do about It* (Princeton, NJ: Princeton University Press, 2011).

6. Studies on high-level thinking similarly show that sensitivity to the occasion to engage in critical thinking is a more important factor than thinking ability. David Perkins, Shari Tishman, Ron Ritchhart, Kiki Donis, and Al Andrade, "Intelligence in the Wild: A Dispositional View of Intellectual Traits," *Educational Psychology Review* 12, no. 3 (September 1, 2000): 269–293.

7. Margo Gardner and Laurence Steinberg, "Peer Influence on Risk Taking, Risk Preference, and Risky Decision Making in Adolescence and Adulthood: An Experimental Study," *Developmental Psychology* 41, no. 4 (July 2005): 625–635; Mary Jo V. Pugh and Daniel Hart, "Identity Development and Peer Group Participation," *New Directions for Child and Adolescent Development* 1999, no. 84 (1999): 55–70.

8. Avner Levin and Patricia Sánchez Abril, "Two Notions of Privacy Online," *Vanderbilt Journal of Entertainment & Technology Law* 11 (2009): 1001–1051.

9. Emily Weinstein, a doctoral student on our research team, recently conducted focus groups with teens who described subtle online behaviors—such as party photos on Facebook and Instagram—designed to make people feel excluded. Similarly, the teens spoke about subtweeting: complaining about a friend or a peer without naming the person, thereby avoiding accountability.

10. Joseph Kahne, Ellen Middaugh, and Danielle Allen, "Youth, New Media and the Rise of Participatory Politics," in *From Voice to Influence: Understanding Citizenship in the Digital Age*, ed. Danielle Allen and Jennifer Light, forthcoming; Clay Shirky, *Here Comes Everybody: The Power of Organizing without Organizations* (London: Allen Lane, 2008); Elisabeth Soep, *Participatory Politics: Next-Generation Tactics to Remake Public Spheres* (Cambridge, MA: MIT Press, 2014).

11. John Suler, "The Online Disinhibition Effect," *Cyberpsychology & Behavior* 7, no. 3 (2004): 321–326; Roger Silverstone, "Proper Distance: Towards an Ethics for Cyberspace," in *Digital Media Revisited: Theoretical and Conceptual Innovations in Digital Domains*, ed. Gunnar Liestol, Andrew Morrison, and Terje Rasmussen, 469–490 (Cambridge, MA: MIT Press, 2003).

12. danah boyd, "Why Youth ♥ Social Network Sites: The Role of Networked Publics in Teenage Social Life," in *Youth, Identity, and Digital Media*, ed. David Buckingham (Cambridge, MA: MIT Press, 2008), 119–142; danah boyd, "Social Network Sites As Networked Publics: Affordances, Dynamics, and Implications," in *A Networked Self: Identity, Community, and Culture on Social Network Sites*, ed. Zizi Papacharissi, 39–58 (New York: Routledge, 2011), http://www.danah.org/papers.

13. Sherry Turkle, "Always-On/Always-on-You: The Tethered Self," in *Handbook of Mobile Communication Studies*, ed. James E. Katz (Cambridge, MA: MIT Press, 2008), 121–137; Sherry Turkle, *Alone Together: Why We Expect More from Technology and Less from Each Other* (New York: Basic Books, 2011).

14. Herman T. Tavani, "The Impact of the Internet on Our Moral Condition: Do We Need a New Framework of Ethics?," in *The Impact of the Internet on Our Moral Lives*, ed. Robert J Cavalier (Albany, NY: SUNY Press, 2005), 230.

15. Luciano Floridi and J. W. Sanders, "Internet Ethics: The Constructionist Values of Homo Poieticus," in *The Impact of the Internet on Our Moral Lives*, ed. Robert J Cavalier (Albany, NY: SUNY Press, 2005), 195–214.

16. Nicholas Negroponte, *Being Digital* (New York: Vintage Books, 1996).

17. Ellen J. Langer, *Mindfulness* (Reading, MA: Perseus Books, 1989); Howard Rheingold, *Net Smart: How to Thrive Online* (Cambridge, MA: MIT Press, 2012); Scott J. Reynolds, "Moral Attentiveness: Who Pays Attention to the Moral Aspects of Life?," *Journal of Applied Psychology* 93, no. 5 (September 2008): 1027–1041.

18. Perkins et al., "Intelligence in the Wild." These components of a thinking disposition mirror James Rest and colleagues' multifaceted conception of morality, which includes moral sensitivity and motivation along with capacities for judgment. James R. Rest, Darcia Narvaez, Muriel J. Bebeau, and Stephen J. Thoma, *Postconventional Moral Thinking: A Neo-Kohlbergian Approach* (Mahwah, NJ: Lawrence Erlbaum, 1999); James R. Rest, Darcia Narvaez, Stephen J. Thoma, and Muriel J. Bebeau, "A Neo-Kohlbergian Approach to Morality Research," *Journal of Moral Education* 29, no. 4 (2000): 381–395.

19. For more details and findings related to our analysis of these thinking types, see Andrea Flores and Carrie James, "Morality and Ethics behind the Screen: Young People's Perspectives on Digital Life," *New Media & Society* 15, no. 6 (2013): 834–852.

20. As we noted in chapter 1, this notion is resonant with Robert Selman's concept of societal perspective taking. Robert L. Selman, "The Relation of Role Taking to the Development of Moral Judgment in Children," *Child Development* 42, no. 1 (March 1, 1971): 79–91.

21. Alice E. Marwick and danah boyd, "I Tweet Honestly, I Tweet Passionately: Twitter Users, Context Collapse, and the Imagined Audience," *New Media & Society*, July 7, 2010.

22. This type of thinking mirrors Howard Gardner's concept of the ethics of roles. Howard Gardner, *Truth, Beauty, and Goodness Reframed: Educating for the Virtues in the Age of Truthiness and Twitter* (New York: Basic Books, 2012).

23. Bazerman and Tenbrunsel, *Blind Spots*.

24. Nancy Tuana, "Conceptualizing Moral Literacy," *Journal of Educational Administration* 45, no. 4 (2007): 364–378.

25. Resources for thinking routines can be found at http://www.visiblethinkingpz. org; see also Ron Ritchhart, Mark Church, and Karin Morrison, *Making Thinking Visible: How to Promote Engagement, Understanding, and Independence for All Learners* (San Francisco: Jossey-Bass, 2011); and Shari Tishman, David N. Perkins, and Eileen Jay, *The Thinking Classroom: Learning and Teaching in a Culture of Thinking* (Boston: Allyn and Bacon, 1995).

26. The suite of educational materials that Facing History and Ourselves has developed for considering both historical and contemporary cases of irresponsibility, hatred, racism, and genocide includes relevant tools. An exemplary exercise involves deep consideration of one's "universe of obligation" and the conditions under which that universe might be widened. Facing History and Ourselves, "Universe of Obligation," n.d., http://www.facing.org/resources/lesson_ideas/udhr-2-universe -obligation-0.

27. Ritchhart et al., *Making Thinking Visible*, 171–177.

28. Richard Weissbourd, "The Bullying Conundrum," *Education*, Fall 2012, http:// www.gse.harvard.edu/news-impact/2012/09/the-bullying-conundrum; Richard Weissbourd, "True Empathy," *Huffington Post*, November 26, 2013, http://www.huffington post.com/richard-weissbourd/true-empathy_b_4330826.html.

29. Lynn Barendsen and Wendy Fischman, "The Good Work Toolkit," Project Zero, Harvard Graduate School of Education, 2010. An online version of the values-sort activity can be found at http://www.thegoodproject.org/good-work/the-good-work -project/the-goodwork-toolkit/value-sort-activity.

30. Daniel Goleman, *Focus: The Hidden Driver of Excellence* (New York: HarperCollins, 2013); Katrina Schwartz, "Age of Distraction: Why It's Crucial for Students to Learn to Focus," *MindShift*, December, 2013, http://blogs.kqed.org/mindshift/2013 /12/age-of-distraction-why-its-crucial-for-students-to-learn-to-focus.

31. Kahne et al., "Youth, New Media and the Rise of Participatory Politics"; Soep, *Participatory Politics*.

32. For an illuminating discussion of how youth manage the positive opportunities and negative challenges associated with voicing civic issues online, see Emily Weinstein, "The Personal Is Political on Social Media: Online Civic Expression Patterns and Pathways among Civically Engaged Youth," *International Journal of Communication* 8 (2014): 210–233.

33. Jaron Lanier, *You Are Not a Gadget: A Manifesto* (New York: Knopf, 2010), 7.

34. Andrés Monroy-Hernández, Benjamin Mako Hill, Jazmin Gonzalez-Rivero, and danah boyd, "Computers Can't Give Credit: How Automatic Attribution Falls Short in an Online Remixing Community," in *Proceedings of the SIGCHI Conference on Human Factors in Computing Systems* (New York: ACM, 2011), 3421–3430.

35. Jason M. Stephens, Michael F. Young, and Thomas Calabrese, "Does Moral Judgment Go Offline When Students Are Online? A Comparative Analysis of Undergraduates' Beliefs and Behaviors Related to Conventional and Digital Cheating," *Ethics & Behavior* 17, no. 3 (2007): 233–254.

36. Further problems with dependence on apps and other technologies for self-expression, intimacy, and creativity are described in Howard Gardner and Katie Davis, *The App Generation: How Today's Youth Navigate Identity, Intimacy, and Imagination in a Digital World* (New Haven, CT: Yale University Press, 2013).

37. Jimmy Soni, "The Reason HuffPost Is Ending Anonymous Accounts," *Huffington Post*, August 26, 2013, http://www.huffingtonpost.com/jimmy-soni/why-is-huffpost -ending-an_b_3817979.html?utm_hp_ref=tw.

38. "Facebook's Online Speech Rules Keep Users on a Tight Leash," *All Things Considered*, NPR, April3, 2013, http://www.npr.org/blogs/alltechconsidered/2013 /04/03/176147408/facebooks-online-speech-rules-keep-users-on-a-tight-leash.

39. Jeffrey Lin and Carl Kwoh, "Play Nice! The Science of Player Behavior in Online Games," MIT Game Lab, March 20, 2013, http://gamelab.mit.edu/event/play-nice -the-science-of-player -behavior-in-online-games.

40. Katie Davis and Carrie James, "Tweens' Conceptions of Privacy Online: Implications for Educators," *Learning, Media and Technology* 38, no. 1 (2013): 4–25.

41. Good Play Project and Project New Media Literacies, *Our Space: Being a Responsible Citizen of the Digital World*, Project Zero, Harvard Graduate School of Education, and Annenberg School of Communication, University of Southern California, 2011, http://dmlcentral.net/sites/dmlcentral/files/resource_files/Our_Space_full_ casebook_compressed.pdf.

42. Common Sense Media, "Digital Literacy and Citizenship Classroom Curriculum," 2011, http://www.commonsensemedia.org/educators/curriculum.

43. Barendsen and Fischman, "The Good Work Toolkit."

44. The finding about the relative absence of adults in the online lives of teens and emerging adults may be related to the fact that we interviewed them in 2008, when adults were largely not participating in social network sites such as Facebook. More recent studies indicate that parents of teens at least believe that they know what their teens are doing online, but it was also found that teens are able to use work-arounds to outsmart their parents and limit knowledge of their true activities. McAfee, "The Digital Divide: How the Online Behavior of Teens Is Getting Past Parents," June 25, 2012, http://www.mcafee.com/us/about/news/2012/q2/20120625-01.aspx. A November 2012 Pew survey indicated that parents' concerns include advertisers' access to information about their children, "stranger danger," how youth manage their reputations online, and the effect of online content on college admissions and employment. Mary Madden, Sandra Cortesi, Urs Gasser, Amanda Lenhart, and Maeve Duggan, *Parents, Teens, and Online Privacy*, Pew Internet and American Life Project, November 20, 2012, http://pewinternet.org/Reports/2012/Teens-and-Privacy.aspx.

45. Davis and James, "Tweens' Conceptions of Privacy Online."

46. Somini Sengupta, "Warily, Schools Watch Students on the Internet," *New York Times*, October 28, 2013, http://www.nytimes.com/2013/10/29/technology/some-schools-extend-surveillance-of-students-beyond-campus.html.

47. Henry Jenkins, "Raising the Digital Generation: What Parents Need to Know about Digital Media and Learning," *Confessions of an Aca-Fan*, October 11, 2010, http://henryjenkins.org/2010/10/raising_the_digital_generation.html.

48. Sam Gilbert, "Ethics at Play: Patterns of Ethical Thinking among Young Online Gamers," in *Ethics and Game Design: Teaching Values through Play*, ed. Karen Schrier and David Gibson (Hershey, PA: IGI Global, 2010), http://www.igi-global.com/bookstore/chapter.aspx?titleid=41317.

49. Mizuko Ito, Sonja Baumer, Matteo Bittanti, danah boyd, Rachel Cody, Becky Herr-Stephenson, Heather A. Horst, et al., *Hanging Out, Messing Around, and Geeking Out: Kids Living and Learning with New Media* (Cambridge, MA: MIT Press, 2010).

50. Mizuko Ito, Kris Gutiérrez, Sonia Livingstone, Bill Penuel, Jean Rhodes, Katie Salen, Juliet Schor, Julian Sefton-Green, and S. Craig Watkins, *Connected Learning: An Agenda for Research and Design* (Irvine, CA: Digital Media and Learning Research Hub, 2013), http://dmlhub.net/sites/default/files/ConnectedLearning_report.pdf.

51. Samantha Stendal, *A Needed Response*, YouTube, March 22, 2013, http://www.youtube.com/watch?v=eZxv5WCWivM.

52. "UO Student's 'Steubenville Trial' Response Video Goes Viral," KVAL, n.d., http://www.kval.com/news/local/UO-students-Steubenville-trial-response-video-goes-viral-199765031.html.

Appendix

1. Carrie James, Katie Davis, Andrea Flores, John M. Francis, Lindsay Pettingill, Margaret Rundle, and Howard Gardner, *Young People, Ethics, and the New Digital Media: A Synthesis from the GoodPlay Project* (Cambridge, MA: MIT Press, 2009).

2. Barney Glaser and Anselm Strauss, *The Discovery of Grounded Theory: Strategies for Qualitative Research* (New Brunswick, NJ: Aldine Transaction, 1967).

Index